what is a loose-head?

The mysteries of rugby union explained

John Griffiths

**ROBSON
BOOKS**

First published in the United Kingdom in 2007 by
Robson Books
10 Southcombe Street
London
W14 0RA

An imprint of Anova Books Company Ltd

Illustrations by Barking Dog Art

ISBN 10: 1 86105 981 7
ISBN 13: 9781861059819

A CIP catalogue record for this book is available from the British Library.

10 9 8 7 6 5 4 3 2 1

Typeset by SX Composing DTP, Rayleigh, Essex
Printed and bound by WS Bookwell, Finland

This book can be ordered direct from the publisher.
Contact the marketing department, but try your bookshop first.

www.anovabooks.com

Contents

	Acknowledgements	vi
1	**Why This Book?**	1
2	**How Did Rugby Union Evolve?**	4
	Did the Greeks (or Romans) have a word for it?	4
	When did games begin?	4
	Who was William Webb Ellis?	5
	How did international matches start?	6
	Where does the International Board fit in?	8
	When was the first Rugby World Cup?	8
	How did the game become professional?	9
3	**What Is Rugby Union?**	11
	On the ball	11
	Is rugby like American football?	12
	Is Rugby League a different game?	13
	How many players are on each side?	13
	How are points scored?	13
	How long does a match last?	17
4	**Which Teams Play the Game?**	18
	International Rugby Union	18
	The Lions	19
	Short tours	19
	Who are the up-and-coming Nations?	20
	European and Super competitions	21
	Other club rugby	22
	What about the Barbarians?	23
	Coarse Rugby	24
	Who are the Golden Oldies?	24
5	**Who Plays Where?**	26
	The pitch	26
	What are the markings on the pitch for?	27
	Touch and throw-ins	28
	What if the ball lands on a line?	31
	Backs and forwards	31
	The backs – what do all the fractions mean?	31
	The forwards and their roles	35
	What are substitutes and replacements?	39

So how are teams numbered?   40

6 **Who Keeps Control of the Players?**   **42**
Referees   42
Sanctions   43
Rugby's unique law   44
Cards, sin-bins and citings   45
The advantage law   45
Offside   46
Safety first   48
Ball touching the referee   49
What does the referee need to carry?   49
Touch judges   50
What's a TMO?   52
Is there an association that represents the interests of   53
  leading players?

7 **What About Tactics?**   **54**
What exactly are tactics?   54
What is open play?   55
How is the tight game played?   58
How do teams defend?   62
Is there a master plan?   66

8 **Everyone Knows Jonny Wilkinson, But Who Was**   **68**
Alex Obolensky?
Jonny Wilkinson   68
Prince Alex Obolensky   69
Who are the other famous names in Rugby Union?   70
What about this Clive Woodward bloke?   86

9 **Twickenham and Other Famous Grounds**   **88**
Twickhenham – the game's Mecca   88
Cardiff   91
Murrayfield   93
Lansdowne Road   95
Stade de France   96
Stadio Olimpico, Rome   97
Ellis Park, Johannesburg   97
Eden Park, Auckland   98

10 **What Media Coverage Does Rugby Get?**   **100**
Which critics and newspapers should I read?   100
What are the important books about the game?   101
Broadcasting   102
Other media   103

Do I need to know any famous statistics?   104

11   So, Am I Ready to Go and Watch a Match Now?   **107**
Getting ready for the game   107
During the game   108
Are all spectators potential streakers?   109

12   What Is Rugby Union's Appeal?   **110**
Glossary   **112**

Acknowledgements

Thanks are due to Jeremy Robson for commissioning this title and for his enthusiasm for the project. Jane Donovan and Ian Allen made helpful suggestions regarding the text, while in-house Nichola Smith's lively design and Barbara Phelan's skilful oversight of the project finally brought the book to life.

1

Why This Book?

In the autumn of 2006 **international** rugby teams from New Zealand, South Africa and Argentina visited Britain and played matches against England, the then reigning world champions. The visitors all succeeded in their quests to topple the country where the game began and, by doing so, they added to the record string of defeats suffered by England's national team in 2006.

Yet for all the disappointments of continued losses, support for rugby in Britain, Ireland and Europe was at record levels. The authorities staging England's home matches rapidly sold out of tickets – indeed they could have filled the stadium at least twice over for the New Zealand and South Africa matches.

Despite the national side's temporary loss of form, interest in the game at club level was rapidly increasing. In December 2006, an all-embracing survey conducted by **Premier Rugby** of 12,000 club rugby supporters in England was published. It showed that 93 per cent of respondents rated rugby at the highest club level as 'good' entertainment. Nearly all (96 per cent) enjoyed its competitiveness.

Two-thirds reckoned the sport offered good value for money and nearly three-quarters rated rugby as good family entertainment. These figures were borne out by another interesting result of the survey: that 34 per cent of spectators at club matches in 2005–6 were parents of children under 16, up from 22 per cent the **season** before. Later in 2006, more than 48,000 turned out at Lansdowne

1

Road in Dublin to watch Ireland's oldest provincial rivals, Leinster and Ulster, meet in a league match.

Then, in February and March 2007, the mean attendance at the fifteen matches in Britain, Ireland, France and Italy's popular **International Championship** was higher than for any football World Cup tournament's final stages. Measured by attendances alone, the old Championship, it could be said, is the most popular sporting event of any kind in the world.

Further confirmation of rugby's growing attraction elsewhere in Britain, Ireland and Europe came the same season when tickets for the sport's **Rugby World Cup**, to be staged in France in September and October 2007, went on sale to the general public. This was the third phase of the ticketing sales for the tournament and the organising committee's website was so inundated with enquiries that it crashed within two hours of opening. By the end of the first day of sales, a third of the 550,000 tickets had been snaffled up and the available allocations for seven of the pool matches sold out.

Apart from the game's rising stock as family entertainment offering value for money, another attraction of rugby is its camaraderie. Friendships formed through playing or regularly watching the game often last a lifetime. The eighty minutes' entertainment on the pitch is followed by after-match rituals that are the envy of other sports.

Yes, sometimes blind eyes are turned to the antics of young and not-so-young followers. But generally rugby is a game that engenders friendly rivalry and innocent banter among players and supporters – there has never been the need to keep rival spectators apart even at the highest level of competition. Rugby is a physical game, yet part of its attraction is that the strongest and most skilful of its players manage to excel without resorting to violence.

To the newcomer, however, it is a complex game and the idea of this book is to unlock some of its mysteries. It attempts to explain rugby's vocabulary and traditions, and to give the uninitiated an idea of how to appreciate the game. It is NOT a 'How-to-Play' book.

The book can be read straight through or dipped into as an 'enquire within'. Each chapter deals with topics on which newcomers to rugby might require some explanation, and an extensive glossary is provided for reference. The first time that a word of rugby jargon appears in the text it is printed in bold so the reader can look it up in the glossary. Finally, apologies to any of the growing number of women players and enthusiasts who might take offence at the male pronouns used in the book. Rugby is predominately a male pastime so the convention is to refer to players and officials as 'he'.

Six Rugby Quotes

Rugby is a game for gentlemen of all classes, but never for a poor sportsman in any class.
— *Bishop Walter Carey, Oxford rugby blue of the 1890s*
I must say that when a **referee** is in doubt, I think he is justified in deciding against the side which makes most noise. They are probably in the wrong.
— *Dr H H Almond, headmaster of Loretto School in Musselburgh near Edinburgh, on his decision to allow a hotly disputed try to Scotland in the first-ever international match, played in Edinburgh in March 1871*
Twickenham is the last fortress of the Forsytes.
— *Ivor Brown*
A bomb under the West Stand on an international day at Twickenham would end fascism in England for a generation.
— *Philip Toynbee*
We may not be the best team in the world, but at least we turn up.
— *John Pullin, England captain, on his team's defeat by Ireland in Dublin in 1973 (Scotland and Wales had declined to play there the year before because of the political troubles)*
In Rugby, you kick the ball; in Association, you kick the man if you cannot kick the ball; and in Gaelic, you kick the ball if you cannot kick the man.
— *Irish journalist Jacques MacCarthy describing the three forms of football played in Ireland in the 1890s . . . more than a hundred years before rugby football was first played on Gaelic football's hallowed turf at Croke Park*

2.
How Did Rugby Union Evolve?

Did the Greeks (or Romans) have a word for it?

Historians confirm that the Greeks (around 400 BC) and later the Romans refer to a team ball game played on a rectangular field with a **halfway line** and **goal lines**. Translations suggest that the game was one involving physical contact, that the ball was transferred from player to player through a **pass** and that there was no **kicking**. The features of the game appear to have remained virtually unchanged for 800 years.

The Latin word for this recreation was **harpastum.** It first appeared in Britain approximately 2,000 years ago, practised by the Roman legions during their occupation.

When did games begin?

In England, the Romans gave way to the Angles and Saxons, and later the Normans, all of whom appear to have enjoyed variations of ball games. By the nineteenth century, many towns and villages in England were enjoying a game called 'football' that had evolved from harpastum but which now involved unlimited numbers. Festival days, such as Shrove Tuesday, were regarded as the traditional time for playing games.

The game evolved differently from town to town, there being no code of playing behaviour or written set of rules. A report of a three-day match at Sheffield in 1793 asserts: 'There were many slightly wounded', but reassuringly adds, 'none killed'.

The aim was for a mob representing one town to force a ball through a target or goal situated in its opponent's town. Play was wild and fierce according to historians and attracted hordes of spectators. These games typically took place at holiday time, Shrove Tuesday games being recorded in the early 1700s in Derby and in Kingston-on-Thames in 1815. At Chester a game was played in commemoration of the day in AD 217 when a mighty flying wedge was organised to banish the Roman legion from the town.

Who was William Webb Ellis?

Modern rugby footballers measure their dates from 1823, when 16-year-old William Webb Ellis caused such a stir by reputedly gathering a ball and running with it at Rugby School in Warwickshire. Ellis's action was regarded as 'not football', but his deed was to give the game of rugby football its distinction as a handling code.

Ellis was probably not the first man to run with a ball at football; it has since been established that his action was the norm in parts of Cornwall and East Anglia in the early nineteenth century. More likely, it was the fact that he performed his feat at a school that was about to undergo a reformation that bestowed lasting fame upon the youngster as the 'inventor' of rugby football.

The immediate consequence of his running with the ball is unknown, and the next protagonist to feature in the development of the game was Dr Thomas Arnold, an innovative educator who became headmaster at Rugby School five years after Ellis's shocking indiscretion.

The English public schools had been founded in the Middle Ages with the aim of preparing pupils for the great universities of Oxford and Cambridge. At first the schools, which were not expressly established for the rich, flourished by providing a free education to pupils with academic potential. But by 1800 the most prominent public schools had fallen into relative decline. They became complacent and the legend grew up that in the pursuit of leisure, public-school pupils indulged in bullying, drinking, poaching, gambling – and even shooting their masters.

Dr Arnold successfully arrested this decline by broadening the curriculum and developing a commitment to character training. Beatings were actively discouraged and a sound classical grounding was imparted with a strong flavour of Christianity. In particular, his encouragement of team games brought about a revolution of the public-school system. His pupils and colleagues had a high regard for him and his ideals, and Rugby School was held up as a model public school.

Through Rugby School's pupils and masters, the Arnold methods and traditions spread to other schools. Disciples of Arnold's methods believed in the emphasis on sporting activity as a suitable occupation for pupils' leisure, and the encouragement of team games was seen as a positive antidote to immorality.

Later, it became evident that the virtues of loyalty, co-operation and esprit de corps were developed through organised school sport and football – the Rugby School variety in particular – was to flourish at the public schools. This spread naturally to the great universities and later more widely as the young men of Rugby and other influential schools took up their careers and travelled the country.

It might be spurious to suggest that William Webb Ellis invented rugby football, but it is true to say that without the combination of Ellis, Dr Arnold and the school that was destined to set the fashion in sport for many other schools, the game would probably never have spread as it did.

How did international matches start?

In 1839, the first club playing the Rugby School rules was formed at Cambridge University by an Old Rugbeian, Arthur Pell. From 1839 to 1846, a succession of public schoolboys joining the club on arriving at Cambridge from the prominent public schools brought a variety of rules to the game of football, no doubt to the great annoyance of Pell and his Rugby cronies.

Old Etonians objected to Rugbeians running with the ball and by 1848 had been instrumental in drawing up the 'Cambridge Rules', which were later adopted by the Football Association at its foundation meeting in 1863, thus marking the parting of the ways between rugby and soccer.

A club devoted to the Rugby School rules was reputedly formed at Guy's Hospital in 1843, while the Blackheath and Richmond rugby clubs were formed in 1862 and 1863 respectively. Oxford University formed its rugby club in 1869, the inaugural rugby match in the north of England was played in 1857 and by the 1860s there were centres established in Manchester and Liverpool.

By December 1870, Old Rugbeian Edwin Ash and other devotees of the rugby code were ready to draft a letter to the press inviting correspondence from interested parties of other clubs with a view to forming a rugby society. The immediate reasons for the formation of such a body were the requirement that a common code of rules should be drafted by a body recognised by all clubs, and also the need for a governing body to arrange and select a side to honour a challenge from Scotland to play an international match.

The upshot of Edwin Ash's initiative was that in January 1871, 21 clubs were represented at the formation of the **Rugby Football Union** (RFU). Old Rugbeians dominated the RFU's early meetings and it was unsurprising that the code of rules drawn up by the fledgling **Union** was, in most respects, a close version of the Rugby School **Laws** of 1871.

The RFU also responded to a challenge issued through the sporting press for an England team to meet Scotland and the first international match was staged in March 1871 in Edinburgh. Before the match, the two sides sat down with the referee to establish the common laws under which the game should be played.

England were led by Fred Stokes. He was only 20 (still the youngest age for an England captain) and, appropriately, an Old Rugbeian like half that original England team. Their uniform comprised white jerseys and white knickerbockers tucked into brown stockings – the colours of Rugby School.

They lost, having travelled through the night before arriving in Edinburgh on the morning of the game. Then, at the ground, they found the pitch on which the match was staged to be considerably narrower than the dimensions they were used to.

England won the return fixture at the Oval in 1872 and by 1873 the side was becoming more representative of the English clubs and public schools. International rugby had become well established and the England–Scotland game was regarded as rugby's match of the year.

Until 1876 matches were twenty-a-side affairs. Then, in 1877, after a successful experiment involving fifteen-a-side teams in the Oxford–Cambridge university match, international teams were reduced. With ten fewer players on the pitch, rugby matches became more entertaining spectacles and began to attract more interest from the general public.

Where does the International Board fit in?

Ireland and Wales entered the international lists in the decade that followed the first England–Scotland match and in 1884, for the first time, each of the four **Home Unions** competed in an unofficial International Championship.

England were champions and won the **Triple Crown** that year, but only through a hotly disputed winning score in the annual showdown with Scotland. The Scots were so annoyed that they refused to meet England a year later and proposed that a board be appointed to settle matters arising from international matches.

The RFU disagreed with Scotland's proposition, fearing the new body would be a threat to its standing in the game. The RFU also argued that it should have a greater representation than the other Home Unions. A meeting did take place in Dublin in 1886 where the Scots 'for the good of the game' accepted the result of the 1884 match, but the RFU refused to participate in a subsequent meeting at Manchester where the **International Rugby Board** (IRB) was set up by the Scottish, Irish and Welsh Unions.

The body's brief was to discuss disputes and formulate policies (particularly relating to the laws of the game) regarding international rugby. When the RFU boycotted the IRB meeting a year later, the other Unions made the English pariahs, kicking them out of the International Championship until three years later, when the RFU changed its stance and accepted an invitation to take a place on the game's ruling body.

Today there are more than one hundred Unions and international bodies in affiliation to the Board.

When was the first Rugby World Cup?

For the best part of the first hundred years after the formation of the Board the only other Unions joining were from the backbone of the British Commonwealth: South Africa, New Zealand and Australia (the so-called **Tri-Nations**). France were belatedly admitted to full membership in 1978.

With never more than eight Unions in membership, talk of World Cups was always dismissed as irrelevant and unviable by the IRB until the early 1980s, when support for a world competition finally gained significant momentum.

In 1987, Australia and New Zealand co-hosted the game's first Rugby World Cup. There were sixteen teams in the tournament that was won by New Zealand. The finalists were invited to take part without any qualification process.

Big oaks from small acorns grow. Twenty years on and the qualification process for the twenty places available in the final stages begins almost as soon as the previous event has been completed. There have been four successful tournaments staged since that inaugural event, with the competition attracting blue-chip sponsors and broadcasters who pour millions of pounds into the IRB's coffers for the future development of rugby worldwide.

Today the Rugby World Cup sits at the top of a pyramid that motivates the IRB's worldwide membership and is the third biggest event after the Olympic Games and soccer's World Cup on world sport's calendar.

Rugby's World Cup winners

1987	New Zealand
1991	Australia
1995	South Africa
1999	Australia
2003	England

How did the game become professional?

Until 1995 Rugby Union was a strictly **amateur** game . . . in theory. Unlike soccer or cricket its players, even at the highest level, were unpaid for their efforts and achievements. It was the game's defining principle.

Inevitably though, there were abuses. As Rugby Union's attraction spread, particularly to commercial enterprises in the latter years of the twentieth century, not unreasonably players pressed to be rewarded for their efforts. After all, it was their skills as entertainers that brought the game sharply into focus and generated huge income for the governing bodies that organised international matches.

Previously players who had made a clean breast of wanting to be paid for playing rugby had had to join the professional ranks of **Rugby League**. Such a move was one way: a player leaving the Union code for the league game could not be reinstated as a Union player. But for years it was suspected that many leading players, particularly those who were in unskilled or low-paid occupations, received **boot money** in reward for their playing services or as an incentive to remain loyal to Rugby Union's ranks. At the same time the game's administrators continued to market the sport as wholesomely amateur – an hypocrisy that was neatly summed up in the word **shamateurism**.

At a meeting of the IRB in Paris in September 1995, its chairman Vernon Pugh QC produced a written report that proposed an end to the folly of abuses. He presented his case with the panoply of skills he had honed in the legal profession and at one fell swoop succeeded in releasing the game from its suffocating and outdated amateur tenets.

IRB members embraced his proposals without even taking a vote on the matter and the game went **open** during the course of one momentous weekend. The upshot was that Rugby League players could now transfer to Union.

Six rugby internationals who played Union after winning League honours

Andy Farrell	England
Iestyn Harris	Wales
Henry Paul	England
Jason Robinson	England
Mat Rogers	Australia
Wendell Sailor	Australia

3.
What Is Rugby Union?

On the ball

Rugby is a game played with a funny-shaped ball. The mathematical name for the shape of a rugby football is an ellipsoid, but most refer to it as the oval ball, while players often call it the **pill**.

One of the fascinations of rugby is the unpredictability of the bounce of the ball. It is the oval shape that gives rise to that uncertainty. At the same time, however, the shape makes it easier to carry and throw.

Nowadays balls comprise four outer panels made from a synthetic substance that makes them easy to handle in wet conditions. The panels surround an air-inflated rubber bladder. The ball's weight must not exceed 440 grams and its major axis must not exceed 30 centimetres. There are also limits on the girth of the ball.

The balls originally used at Rugby School in the 1820s and 1830s were made of leather panels enclosing a raw pig's bladder, which gave them a more spherical appearance than today's modern examples. The bladder had to be inflated by mouth, a rather unpleasant exercise that was expertly performed by a Mr Gilbert, who ran a ball-making business in Rugby's town centre. The Gilbert business passed from the family only relatively recently, but to this day the name adorns the balls that are used in major international matches.

Senior matches are played with a size-five rugby ball. Size four is used in junior school matches while a size-three ball is used in **mini-rugby**.

Is rugby like American football?

Historians believe that American football evolved from the English public-school game of rugby football, and there are a number of similarities between the sports. An understanding of American football helps newcomers understand Rugby Union.

Both American football and rugby are played with an oval ball, the rugby version being slightly larger (and therefore more difficult to control) than the American football. Like the American game, the prime object of rugby is to move forward with the ball and force a **touchdown** or **try** resulting in **points** being added to a team's score. Points can also be scored by kicking a **goal**. The winning team is the one that scores the majority of points.

To gain ground, players with the ball are allowed to run with it, kick it or pass it. Moreover, both games involve physical contact. Players can prevent opponents gaining ground with the ball by making a **tackle**. They are also allowed to take the ball from an opponent. The team with the ball aims to retain its **possession**, while the team without the ball usually aims to **turnover** possession.

Six Differences Between Rugby Union and American Football

* American footballers wear crash helmets, shoulder pads and body protectors. Rugby players wear jockstraps – they know their priorities.
* The American football is smaller than the rugby ball, making it easier to throw, while the rugby pitch is wider.
* Rugby players pass the ball sideways or backwards, but not forwards.
* Rugby teams are not permitted to call time-outs.
* Blocking is a legal tactic in American football; it is called obstruction in Rugby Union.
* There are more players (fifteen) in a Rugby Union team than in an American football team (eleven), though the mass substitutions allowed in the American version gives it the appearance of a cast of thousands.

Is Rugby League a different game?

Oh, yes. Originally there was only one game called rugby. By the 1890s, however, many players in the north of England, where the game was largely played by working men, wanted payment for travelling time spent away from their jobs.

The RFU ruled that the game should remain strictly amateur, leading to discontent among the northern clubs, who split away from the RFU to form the Northern Union. Originally the Northern game was played to the same laws.

Eventually the Northern Union administrators set their game on a different path from the Union officials. They reduced the number of players, set up competitive leagues and removed some of the traditional features of the Union game. The Northern Union evolved into Rugby League and continues as an alternative to Rugby Union to this day, despite Union itself becoming a **professional game** in 1995.

How many players are on each side?

Rugby Union is a game played by two teams, each with fifteen players. A team – sometimes referred to as a **fifteen** – can nominate **substitutes** or **replacements** who sit on the **bench** and await a call to take part, but at any given time during a match only fifteen players are allowed on the pitch.

Sevens is an abbreviated form of the game that was invented in Scotland as an end-of-season party for a collection of local clubs. Today it is almost as big a money-spinner as the full version of the game, with the IRB organising an annual international circuit of tournaments as well as a four-yearly Sevens World Cup.

How are points scored?

The aim of the game is to score points from tries and goals. There are four scoring actions in Rugby Union – three types of goal and a try. Goals are scored by kicking the ball through the **posts** and above the **crossbar**. A goal is still scored if the ball goes over the crossbar and is then blown back into the **field of play**, or if it strikes an upright or the crossbar before going through.

A try occurs when a player **grounds the ball** behind an opponent's goal line. The value of a try is five points. The ball can be grounded by holding it in the hands or arms and bringing it into contact with the opponents' **in-goal** area, by putting the hands on the ball with downward pressure when it is lying in the in-goal area or by falling on it with any part of the front of the body between shoulders and waist.

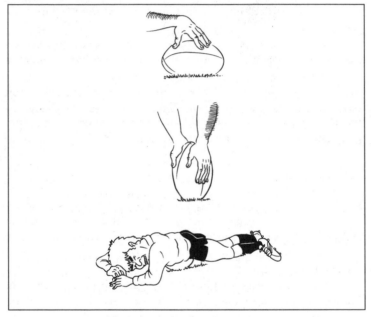

Three ways of grounding the ball

After a try is scored, the scorer's team attempts to add a goal called a **conversion** worth two points. The kick for the conversion can be taken from any point on a line through the point where the try was awarded and parallel to the **touchline**. The posts are imagined to extend infinitely in a vertical direction, so that if a kicker sends the ball above the natural height of the uprights, a goal can still be awarded. The type of kick can be a place kick or drop kick, though usually the former is preferred in fifteen-a-side rugby. In Sevens, however, all conversions must be taken with drop kicks.

opposition may advance from their goal-line when the kicker starts his run-up

Taking a Conversion

Six famous tries

1958 Peter Jackson's lung-bursting corner try on the stroke of time to clinch victory for England against Australia at Twickenham.

1965 Andy Hancock to save the match for England against Scotland at Twickenham in the last minute of the game.

1973 Gareth Edwards for the Barbarians against New Zealand at Cardiff Arms Park. Arguably the most famous try of all time.

1987 Serge Blanco, also in the last minute, for France against Australia in Sydney to win the semifinal at the first Rugby World Cup.

1991 Philippe Saint-André for France against England in a **Grand Slam** showdown at Twickenham. The move had started from the French dead-ball line.

1994 Jean-Luc Sadourny's last-minute 'try from the end of the world' was another ambitious French effort from deep inside their own half. This one won the match against New Zealand in Auckland and sealed a 2–0 Test series win for France over the All Blacks.

A **penalty try** is awarded whenever, but for **foul play** or repeated infringement by the opposing team, a try would, in the opinion of the referee, probably have been scored. In such cases the referee will award the try between the posts, making the conversion attempt straightforward.

A **penalty goal** is scored after certain types of infringement. Its value is three points. The kicker needs to inform the referee of his intention to attempt a goal and the kick is taken from the place where the infringement occurred or on a line drawn behind it parallel to the touchlines. Infringing teams must retire ten metres from the place of infringement and remain still while the kick at goal is taken.

A **drop goal** is scored when a player propels the ball over his opponent's goal by means of a **drop kick**. It is also worth three points and can be scored from any point in the field of play.

Six Rugby Luvvies

Richard Burton Famous Welsh actor who once gave a matinee performance of *Hamlet* on a London stage while trying to follow an England–Wales match at Twickenham. Stage crew in the wings held up large boards every time the score changed.

Oliver Reed Well-known Rosslyn Park rugby club regular and hell-raiser who also enjoyed the occasional drink.

Ross Kemp The former *EastEnders* tough guy was a regular with London clubs Brentwood, Saracens and Maidstone in his playing days.

Boris Karloff He had the build to fill his opponents with horror – in the *Frankenstein* films as well as on the rugby pitch. Karloff founded the Southern Californian Rugby Union in the mid-1930s.

Richard Harris A talented player in his youth, he once auditioned for a part as a three-quarter in the Irish international team – for which he was a serious contender. Later a well-known rebel-rouser on Cardiff rugby weekends with his contemporaries Richard Burton and Peter O'Toole.

Gerard Depardieu The French connection in this select band of rugby's actors. A very keen follower of his country's game, he was typecast in the role of Santini, the coach of the condom-factory rugby team in the film *The Closet*.

How long does a match last?

Rugby matches at senior level are divided into two **halves** of forty minutes. There is a ten-minute **half-time** pause at the end of the first half while players leave the field to rest and receive revised playing instructions from their **coach**.

At most levels the referee is the sole judge of time, but increasingly at senior level responsibility for ensuring that matches run their course is in the hands of a third **official** who will stop the clock when the referee is attending to an injury or talking to players.

The referee is not allowed to whistle for half-time or **no-side** until the ball becomes **dead**. If a try has been scored or a penalty given when time is up, play must continue until the ball next goes dead. Players are not allowed to make the ball dead by deliberately throwing it out of the field of play.

Added time (formerly known as **injury time**) is the time added on for such stoppages, so that playing time is precisely forty minutes each half. A **siren** sounds when play has run its full length at the ends of each half.

Before the match starts the rival captains **toss** a coin for the privilege of choosing which half of the field they will defend (or, if they prefer, they can choose to take the **kickoff**). Teams change ends for each half to experience equal measures of the weather conditions.

4.

Which Teams Play the Game?

International Rugby Union

The most popular and attractive version of Rugby Union is the international game. The ambition of every young player today is to win a Rugby World Cup medal for his country in the four-yearly tournament – the game's premier event – staged by the IRB.

New Zealand's **All Blacks**, Australia's **Wallabies** (twice), South Africa (the **Springboks)** and England are the only nations to have won the World Cup's **Webb Ellis Trophy**, nicknamed '**Old Bill**' after William Webb Ellis. These four and the **Tricolores** of France (twice losing finalists) are rugby's leading international teams.

The three southern hemisphere winners have, since 1996, played an annual round robin of games in a tournament known as the Tri-Nations. The games take place in the southern hemisphere's winter.

During the northern hemisphere's winter, England meet Scotland, Ireland and Wales annually to play in a tournament that dates back to the 1880s. Originally known as the International Championship, this competition became the **Five Nations** in 1910, when France first met each of the Home Unions. Italy joined in 2000, since when the annual championship has been referred to as the **Six Nations**.

Only since 1993, when a special trophy was commissioned for presentation to the champions, has there been an official International Championship. Prior to that, all championship tables, title winners, Triple Crown and Grand Slam holders were the inventions of the British, Irish and French press.

The Lions

The year 1910 also marked the beginning of fully representative **tours** by the **British and Irish Lions**. This team is the cream of the rugby-playing talent in the four Home Unions and visits South Africa, Australia and New Zealand in rotation, playing typically a dozen or so matches including a **series** of three games (**Tests**) against the host nation.

The earliest tours took place in the 1880s. In these early years of the game the players who took part were usually those of private means who could afford to be away from their jobs for the six months or so that was involved in sailing to the other side of the world and playing a lengthy list of fixtures.

For the past hundred years, however, the Lions selectors have begun their search for potential **tourists** at least twelve months before the visit and nowadays the tours take place every four years – and exactly halfway between World Cup tournaments.

The Lions have a disappointing record overseas, having only won back-to-back series in the early 1970s. They beat New Zealand in 1971 (for the only time to date) and were invincible in South Africa in 1974.

The nickname 'Lions' dates from the 1920s and derives from the lion badges the tourists gave as mementos to hosts and team followers. The team's kit varied until 1950 when the convention of red shirt (Wales), white shorts (England), blue socks (Scotland) and green stocking flash (Ireland) was adopted.

Short tours

Since 1958, when France undertook a brief visit to South Africa, short Test tours have been the order of the day among the major nations in seasons either side of Lions tours and World Cup tournaments. These usually take place in November (the autumn internationals) in the northern hemisphere and in June in the southern hemisphere. Their purpose is to enable the host nations to prepare for their Six Nations and Tri-Nations events, but for this reason they have become little more than trial games with the major Unions quite often using them as opportunities to blood new players and give experienced squad members a rest.

In early 2007, however, came interesting news that the IRB is planning in the near future to make these November/June tour Tests more purposeful. It is likely that the fixture lists for these matches will be structured in such a way as to provide a seeding scheme for use at the 2011 Rugby World Cup. This will provide much-needed impetus to the June/November Test matches, encouraging participating nations to field their strongest available teams in order to win the highest seedings (and therefore theoretically gain the easiest passage to the final) for the world's premier rugby tournament.

Who are the up-and-coming Nations?

The Five Nations and Tri-Nations are the senior members of the IRB. Italy (**Azzurri**), Argentina (**Pumas**), Canada (**Canucks**) and Japan (**Cherry Blossoms**) follow in seniority and are recognised as Executive Council members of the Board. Among the top twenty international sides are the three Pacific Islands – Tonga, Fiji and Samoa – where the game dates back to the 1920s at international level. Romania (the **Oaks**) and Georgia are the other leading European nations, Uruguay (**Teros**) are second only to Argentina in South America, and Namibia follow South Africa on the African continent.

The United States (**Eagles**) and Russia jockey to hold a place among the top twenty. Regarded as the game's 'sleeping giants', the two superpowers have never managed to match their political power with prowess on the rugby field.

All told there are more than a hundred nations in membership of the IRB and most compete in the qualifying stages for the Rugby World Cup. Zimbabwe, Spain, Portugal and the Ivory Coast, however, are the only minnows to date who have succeeded in reaching the final stages of the tournament.

Many of the leading nations field **sub-international** teams labelled 'A' or 'B'. With encouragement and financial support from the IRB, many A teams compete against the full international sides of slightly weaker nations. An example is the **Churchill Cup**. This annual tournament features Canada and the United States, together with England A (more recently labelled the **Saxons**) and A sides from the other Home Unions.

European and Super competitions

There are thriving competitions just below international level that attract large attendances in Europe and the Tri-Nations. These tournaments took off shortly after Rugby Union went open and became a professional game in 1995.

The **Super 14**, previously known as the Super 6, Super 10 and Super 12 (until 2007), involves the leading South African, New Zealand and Australian provincial teams in a round-robin tournament that leads to semifinals and a final. Television rights payroll the tournament, which typically begins early in the southern hemisphere season (in February).

New Zealand teams have dominated to date. Auckland (the Blues) and Canterbury (the Crusaders) won eight of the first ten professional competitions, with the ACT Brumbies (from Australia) interrupting the duopoly twice. South Africa produced their first winner in 2007.

Matches are played every weekend and provide the Tri-Nations with a wonderful opportunity to measure the skills and talents of their players over a three-month period of intense competition. By the time the final is played at the end of May, each nation is ready to announce its squads for their home internationals (staged in June) before the Tri-Nations internationals begin in July.

So the top performers in the Tri-Nations have a coherent progression of challenges during their season. Many argue that the system helps to explain why Australia and New Zealand in particular have dominated international rugby for most of rugby's professional era, and that it is one the northern hemisphere nations should aspire to.

In Europe, the season is not quite so well structured. The equivalent of the Super 14 is the **Heineken Cup**. This is the **European Cup** for Britain, Ireland, France and Italy's leading clubs, provinces or regions. The French, English and Italians are represented by the top clubs from their equivalent of England's

Premiership. The Irish, Welsh and Scots – the so-called Celtic Fringe – are represented by provincial or regional sides. England and France have thriving club cultures whereas the others are centrally funded.

There is a second-tier tournament called the **European Challenge Cup** for the teams that finish in the lower halves of their respective national leagues. This competition runs in parallel with the main tournament.

The season is fragmented. The Euro tournaments typically occupy pairs of weekends in October, December and January and reach their pinnacles with finals in May. In between, teams return to their home leagues. The Premiership is the domestic focus for the English clubs and a similar league runs in France for their top clubs. The Irish, Scottish and Welsh provinces and regions join forces to play out an annual round robin known as the **Celtic League.**

For the top European players there are also interruptions in November for the autumn internationals and in February and March for the Six Nations tournament.

State of the Unions in the Six Nations

England	Twelve fully professional clubs
France	Thirty fully professional clubs
Ireland	Four professional provincial teams
Italy	Ten professional clubs
Scotland	Three professional regional teams
Wales	Four professional regional teams

Other club rugby

Only the top clubs in England, France and Italy are professionally run and take part in the major tournaments outlined above. The professional game is the tip of Rugby Union's iceberg, involving only 1 per cent of the game's players.

The leading dozen or so club sides elsewhere, in the British Isles and abroad, are semi-professional and stand at the top of complex league systems that vary only very slightly from country to country.

Below them are the myriad leagues where the majority of rugby's amateur players perform every weekend of the season.

It is through these clubs that many of the leading younger players first make their names. Similarly, when top players begin to lose their shine as professionals, they invariably play out their careers happily reverting to the lesser clubs, helping to nurture blossoming talent who benefit from the skills the former professionals bring from their experience at the top levels.

It is through joining a rugby club, usually as social members, that the public has the opportunity of applying for tickets to Rugby Union's major occasions such as international matches. Because tickets for such games are in huge demand, the various international bodies that control the game could fill their stadiums two or three times over for tour Tests or Six Nations matches.

The unions therefore give first refusal for international tickets to their **affiliated** clubs, who in turn offer them to their paid-up members.

What about the Barbarians?

Arguably the world's most famous rugby club is the **Barbarians**. It is a club that has no home: players are invited to take part in its matches on an ad hoc basis and it has been going strong since 1891. The club picks its players from the cream of world rugby. Those selected to turn out for the club consider the invitation a great honour.

Because it has no home, all its matches are effectively tour games. The club's touring traditions grew out of the annual Christmas and Easter tours that were initiated during the early years of the twentieth century. The growing demands on top players' time – particularly in the later amateur days and since the game became professional – seemed to herald the end of the road for the **Baa-Baas**.

The club, however, survives and sticks to its touring traditions to this day, providing international opposition for the Home Unions as well as for major touring international teams. In the past fifty years the club has been instrumental in spreading rugby's gospel first to Canada and more recently to Zimbabwe, South America and Eastern Europe. And in 2007, to celebrate fifty years of its first overseas tour, the club made an ambitious visit to rugby's outposts in North Africa, where a match was arranged against Tunisia.

Coarse Rugby

For those who do not aspire to the professional game, or even to representing their club in league competitions, there is a thriving branch of the sport often referred to as **Coarse Rugby**. Here the players use a match as the excuse for a post-match (or even pre-match) social occasion.

Coarse Rugby matches are invariably shorter, less formal versions of the game. The referee (when there is one) will have a rudimentary grasp of the laws, and there certainly won't be a touch judge present.

Who are the Golden Oldies?

For many players, reaching the age of 35 or 40 means the end of their playing careers. Most are happy to retreat from the pitch and take up positions propping up the club bar and consuming vast volumes of alcohol, reliving past playing glories and telling younger players that the game isn't like it used to be.

For some, however, the thrill of running with the ball and scoring tries never wanes. For these players there exist **Golden Oldies** tournaments worldwide that provide an opportunity for past players to be reunited – on as well as off the field – to show off faded playing skills. These, too, are mainly social occasions, but even in the 50-plus age group fierce, competitive urges are often seen. The classic annual tournament is staged in Bermuda and continues to attract large entries and even larger attendances.

Six fictional works featuring Rugby Union

Tom Brown's Schooldays Thomas Hughes's novel (first published in 1857) recreating the Rugby School of the author's youth. The book includes a remarkably detailed description of how rugby football was played in its early days.

England, Their England A G Macdonnell's classic story, published in 1933, of Scotsman Donald Cameron's search for material about the English character between the wars. The rugby element is an evocative account of a December day out to the annual Oxford–Cambridge Varsity match at Twickenham.

Any Human Heart William Boyd's 2002 novel is one of his most enjoyable works. The fictitious journal describes Logan Mountstuart's experiences of playing hooker in a school match: 'The two packs would face each other . . . a 32-legged, human beetle trying to evacuate an oval leather ball.'

Paddington In Touch Michael Bond's loveable bear goes back to see a match at his old school and gets roped in to play for the Peruvian second XV in this 1989 adventure.

How Green Was My Valley Richard Llewellyn's 1939 classic tale of Welsh valley life includes the inevitable rugby match. Was the fictional fullback, Cyfartha Lewis, the forerunner of the great J P R Williams, perhaps?

The Ordeal of Young Tuppy P G Wodehouse's love of cricket and Rugby Union stemmed from his days as a pupil at Dulwich College. In this 1930 story from *Very Good, Jeeves*, Bertie's friend Tuppy Glossop is besotted with a young lady and wants to impress her by playing rugby. Tuppy reveals a hitherto unknown aspect of his character while playing for his village in a grudge match that 'had certain features not usually seen on the football field'.

5.
Who Plays Where?

The pitch

The game is played on a rectangular pitch measuring up to 100 metres from goal line to goal line and up to 70 metres wide. This area is the field of play and pitches should be marked out as near as possible to these maximum dimensions. In the middle of each goal line is an H-shaped goal. The goal comprises two uprights just over 5½ metres apart with a crossbar 3 metres above the ground.

There is an additional region beyond each goal line called the in-goal area where touchdowns are made. This area runs the width of the pitch and varies in depth from as little as 5 metres to a maximum of 22 metres (depending on the space available).

The end lines running the width of the pitch are called **dead-ball lines.** The lines that mark the perimeter of the pitch lengthways are called touchlines and the in-goal extensions of the touchlines beyond the field of play are called the **touch-in-goal** lines.

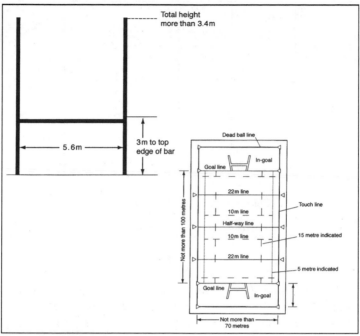

The goal and the pitch

What are the markings on the pitch for?

The pitch is marked by a series of lines that are parallel to its length and width. The central line running the width of the pitch is a line of symmetry so far as the markings are concerned and is called the halfway line. It is from the middle of this line that the kickoff that starts or restarts a game after a score or **half-time** is made.

Running the width of the pitch either side of and parallel to the halfway line are the **10-metre lines**. The team receiving the ball from a kickoff at halfway must stand behind this line until the ball has been kicked. Moreover, the team that kicks off must propel the ball beyond this line before touching it again, unless an opponent has touched it first. If this law is infringed, or the kicker sends the ball straight into touch, the team that receives the kickoff can request a **scrum** on the halfway line, take a **line-out** where the ball entered touch or have the kick taken again.

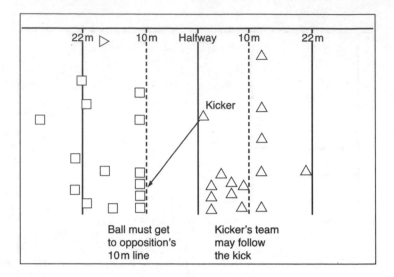

The kick-off

The other pair of lines running the width of the pitch are known as the **22-metre lines,** often shortened to '**22**'. They roughly divide the pitch into quarters, being 22 metres from the goal lines. The **defending team** restarts play from this line by means of a drop kick after it has touched the ball down in its own in-goal area following a kick by an opponent. If, however, the defending side has carried or kicked the ball into its own in-goal area before touching it down, the attacking side is awarded a scrum 5 metres from the defending side's goal line.

Touch and throw-ins

Players are permitted to kick the ball directly into **touch** from any part of the pitch. The game is then restarted by means of a line-out, where typically between two and seven players from each side line up parallel to their goal lines in order to win the ball, which is thrown between them at right angles to the touchline. The opposing side dictates how many players take part in the line-out and has the privilege of taking the **throw-in**, giving it the advantage of choosing where to direct the ball.

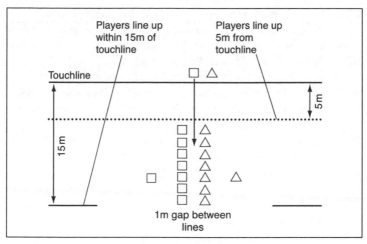

The Line-out

When the player kicks directly to touch from outside his 22-metre line, the line-out takes place on the touchline adjacent to the place where the kick was made. Otherwise, or if the player manages to kick the ball so that it bounces in the field of play before crossing the touchline, the throw-in takes place from the point where the ball crossed the touchline.

Kicking to touch: from a catch, a penalty or a free kick

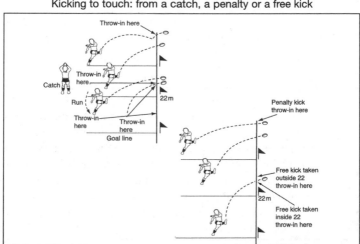

If the ball goes into touch-in-goal play restarts through a 22-metre drop-out to the defending side (if the attacking side is responsible for the stoppage) or a **scrum-five** feed to the attackers (if the defending side caused the stoppage).

Perpendicular to the goal lines are pairs of broken lines that run the length of the pitch. These are the **5-metre lines** and **15-metre lines**. As their names suggest, they are at distances of 5 and 15 metres from the touchlines and are for the guidance of players taking part in the line-out. Throw-ins must travel beyond the 5-metre line, but players at the tail of the line-out can step outside the 15-metre line to collect a long throw-in, provided they do so after the ball has left the thrower's hands. Players throwing in must not step into the field of play, otherwise the throw (or the option of a scrum feed) is given to the opposition.

Players in the line-out usually stand in parallel lines between the 5- and 15-metre lines before the ball is thrown in at right angles to the touchline. The exception to this law is when a team takes a **quick throw-in**. Here the only restrictions are that the ball used is the one that went into touch, that the throw takes place between the thrower's goal line and where the ball crossed the line and that only the thrower has retrieved it or handled it before the throw-in takes place. The throw-in must still travel perpendicular to the touchline.

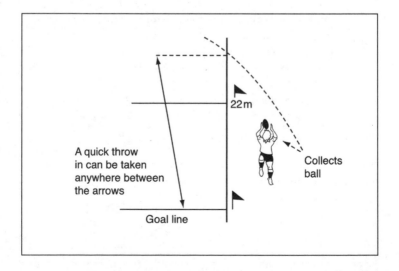

22 m

A quick throw
in can be taken
anywhere between
the arrows

Collects
ball

Goal line

What if the ball lands on a line?

In rugby, the golden rule is that '**on–the–line** is behind the line'. So if a ball lands on a touchline or is touched down by an attacking player on the opposition's goal line, it is regarded as being behind that line for law interpretations and the referee will whistle for a line-out or a try respectively.

Backs and forwards

The fifteen is divided into two sections, the **backs** and the **forwards**.

The backs conventionally take up positions behind the forwards. Their job is to defend when the opposition has the ball, and to create tries in attack, by running, passing or kicking when they have possession. Forwards are chosen for their ability to win the ball when the game is restarted after an infringement or retain it if play breaks down.

The backs are usually slim, fast operators with the ability to beat their opponents through sheer pace, sleight of hand or tricky running – or, ideally, a combination of all three skills. The showmen of the team, the runners and handlers in the backs, are sometimes referred to as the **piano-players**.

The forwards bear the brunt of the heavy contact that goes with competing for the ball. They are typically bigger in build than the backs but not so swift about the pitch. Much of their hard work is unseen, behind the scenes as it were, and for this reason they are referred to as the **piano-shifters**.

Nowadays, the top teams such as the All Blacks, the Wallabies and France possess players who are multi-skilled; athletes who arc able to operate as forwards or backs as the need arises.

The backs – what do all the fractions mean?

Anyone on good terms with the numbers between nought and one will quickly understand why fractions are used to denote the individual positions occupied by the backs.

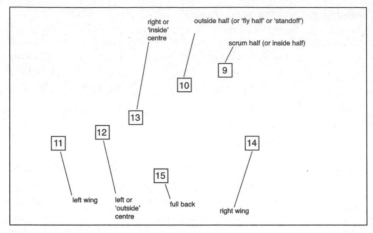

The back division

The halves

There are two **halfbacks**. They stand halfway between their forwards (in front) and the remaining backs (behind them). They form the pivot of the team between the **pack** and the **three-quarters**.

The **scrum half** or **inside half,** who stands nearest to the pack, provides the link between the forwards and remaining backs. The scrum half's duties include putting the ball into the scrum and collecting it from his pack in order to transfer it quickly to his halfback partner or launch an attack himself by running at the opposition. He needs to be sturdy on his legs as well as brave in order to stand his ground in the face of advancing forwards.

The speed of the scrum half's pass is a vital asset to a team. He will therefore use one of two methods for quickly transferring the ball to his team-mates. The **dive pass** is perfected by launching the body off the ground and almost parallel to it, simultaneously projecting the ball to a team-mate. The thinking behind this type of pass is that some of the impulse gained by diving is then transferred to the ball, speeding up its delivery.

Nowadays, however, the **spin pass** has almost universally superseded the dive pass as the preferred method of service from the scrum half. The transfer is not necessarily as quick, but by rolling the wrists over the ball the scrum half sends it spiralling through the air, adding length to his **service**. The result is that his team-mates can stand further away from the passer and hence further away from the attentions of the opposition. Another advantage of the spin pass is that the scrum half remains on his feet and does not lose time through having to pick himself up off the ground.

The other halfback stands off from the forwards in order to 'fly' onto the pass from the scrum half. He is called the **outside half** or **fly half, stand-off half** or, in Ireland, the **out-half**. This is the man who usually decides if the team will advance by means of a passing movement, by running at the opposition himself in order to make a **break**, or by kicking.

Because the outside half is fairly close to the opposition, **heavy traffic** is usually encountered when he receives possession from a set piece. Consequently he has barely a split second in which to weigh up his options and decide what course of action the team will take. He therefore needs to be decisive and a quick thinker.

The three-quarters

The three-quarters line up between the halfbacks and the last line of **defence**, so that they are 'three-quarters' of the way back from the forwards. There are four of these, two **centres** and two **wings**. The centres receive the ball from the outside half in passing movements. If the ball has been transferred swiftly from the forwards, by the time the centres have possession there should be less traffic and therefore more field space available for them to decide what course an attack should take. They need to be strong and resourceful, able to **ride** a tackle and **flat-foot** opponents by rapidly changing the angle of an attack.

Beyond them and near to the touchlines lie the wings, the fastest players on the team. Ideally, the centres transfer the ball as quickly and accurately as possible to these players so they have plenty of space to accelerate onto the ball and race away to score spectacular tries.

Nowadays centres specialise to such an extent that the **inside centre** is the one who always stands next to the outside half, while the **outside centre** lies between him and the wing, whether play is progressing parallel to the left or right touchline. In the past, however, the centres were strictly positioned on the left or right of the field, so that the outside half could find a different player next to him depending on which side of the field his team chose to attack or defend.

The skills required of the inside centre resemble those for the outside half. He needs to have a sharp eye for an opening in attack and the full range of tactical kicking skills in defence. The outside centre has to have a good vision for the game. It is easy for passing movements to suffer from **lateral running**, whereby the direction of attack drifts sideways and little, if any, ground is made. It is the outside centre who is expected to realise this failing and **straighten the line**. This he achieves either by running parallel to the touchline or even at an inwards angle to cause the **drift defence** (that is most effective against lateral running) to change its strategy.

As their names suggest, the **left wing** and **right wing** generally stick to their respective touchlines throughout a match.

Fullback

The last of the backs – often referred to as the last line of defence – is the **fullback**. His multiple purposes are to tackle, catch and kick under pressure in defence and to run the ball, either by joining the **three-quarter line** or initiating moves from the back in attack.

What are five-eighths?

In New Zealand, the back division evolved in a slightly different way. Their system never admitted the left centre/right centre pairing that was so common to European rugby for the best part of the first hundred or so years that the game was played. From the word go, the All Blacks lined up with the same player on the outside half's shoulder – the inside centre of modern parlance.

Recognising that there were always the same two players between the scrum half and three-quarters, the New Zealanders, with arithmetic accuracy, chose to call these two players the **five-eighths** – the fraction that lies exactly halfway between a half and three-quarters.

On the New Zealand system then the scrum half is called *the* halfback; the outside half is known as the **first five-eighth** and the inside centre as the **second five-eighth**.

The All Blacks contended that their system was more versatile and added depth to their attack. Their system was adopted by the other South Pacific rugby-playing nations and eventually, in the light of the successes enjoyed by those nations that used the first/second five-eighths formation, it was adopted (as the outside half/inside centre combination) by the rest of the world.

The forwards and their roles

What is a hooker?

The forwards are chosen for their specialisms at the set pieces: the line-outs and scrums. The scrum is a means of restarting the game after a technical infringement. It is the aspect of rugby that most distinguishes it from other sports. The scrum is a huddle involving the packs of both sides, lined up in three ranks or rows to allow the ball to be put on the ground along a middle line or **tunnel** directly under the shoulders where the two **front rows** meet.

The front rows interlock at a scrummage in such a way that no player's head is next to the head of a player from the same side. To stabilise, the scrum forwards have to **bind** – grasp one another by wrapping their hands and arms around the body of a team-mate.

The front row comprises three specialists: the two **props** and a **hooker**. Yes, there really is a hooker in every rugby team.

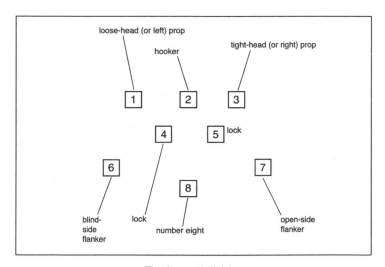

The forward division

35

The hooker is the middle man of the front row and his task is to **strike** for the ball when it appears in the tunnel. The idea is to **heel** the ball so that it moves behind the hooker through the feet of the other rows of the scrum until it emerges for his scrum half to get the rest of back division moving in attack. If the ball is not heeled at the scrum and so fails to emerge from the tunnel, the referee orders a fresh scrum. Players in the scrum are not allowed to kick the ball.

Hookers need strong shoulder and neck muscles in order to bear the pressure on front-row players in scrums, and they have to be agile to use their feet to heel the ball in the very cramped conditions that exist in the front row. They also need to be accurate throwers, for they invariably double up as the player who throws the ball into the line-out, although any player is allowed to do so.

What is the difference between a tight-head and a loose-head?

The two props are supporters of the jumpers in the line-out and hold up the hooker in the scrum. The scrum half always **feeds** the scrum from his hooker's left side. The hooker's left prop, the **loose-head**, always has his left shoulder on the outside of the scrum. As a result, the loose-head only contributes stability in the scrums with his right shoulder, though he must still bind with both arms – the outside binding connecting with his opponent.

Significantly, he and his hooker are half a body's width closer to their scrum half than their immediate opponents, giving the hooker whose side has the feed a clear advantage when striking for the ball. That is why the team that feeds the scrum usually wins the ball.

The prop on the right of the hooker and furthest from the scrum half is called the **tight-head**. His is one of the most difficult positions in the scrum because at all times he is completely locked between the shoulders of his opposing hooker and loose-head prop. It is the pressure that he can exert that occasionally results in a strike **against the tight-head**: that is, winning the ball when the opposite scrum half feeds the scrum.

The tight-head directs his attention at separating the opposition hooker from his loose-head, thereby disrupting their strike in the scrums. For front-row players the tight-head count is the most important statistic in the game – even more important than the actual match result!

Who are the locks?

Behind the front row of the scrum is a line of four forwards forming the **second row**. The two players in the middle of this rank are the **lock** forwards. They tighten – literally lock together – the entire scrum.

Their duties also include jumping for the ball at the line-out, so they are invariably the tallest members of the team, although jumping is not the art it was. Nowadays, players have to stand a metre apart from team-mates in the line-out and there has to be a clear gap down the middle between the opposing jumpers. More significantly, for the past decade or so forwards have been allowed to support jumpers, provided the support is above waist level and occurs after the ball has left the thrower's hands.

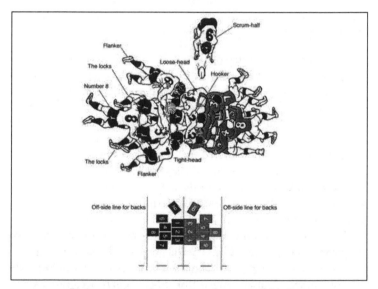

Birds-eye view of a scrum and scrum offside lines

If the hooker throwing in is accurate, that means that the aerial contest at the line-out can quite often take place some 10 to 12 feet above the ground. That makes policing the line-out an easier task for the referee for the simple reason that he can see more clearly what is going on.

Matters were very different until the 1990s. The line-out was regarded as a cover for all kinds of skulduggery and the situation was so ridiculous that a referee could (and often would) find an offence at every throw-in. Arguably, making support legal has tidied up one of the scruffiest aspects of the old game.

The locks are referred to as the engine-room of the pack and are expected to get their legs pumping in unison to provide drive in **rucks**. Moreover, they use their upper-body strength to rip the ball free from opponents at **mauls**.

The front row and locks are referred to collectively as the **front-five**. These are the forwards who bind tightest in the scrums, rucks and mauls. Watch their knuckles turn white as their grips tighten to brace themselves against the opposition's drive or to provide stability for their own shove.

What are flankers and number eights?

The **flankers** or **wing forwards** attach themselves to the side of the scrum outside the two locks in the second row. They are the team's destroyers. In defence their prime duty is to break off the scrum as soon as the ball emerges and make beelines for the opposition in order to snuff out potential attacks. In attack the flankers are expected to support and protect players so that if a team-mate is tackled the ball can be recycled for another attack to be launched.

To perform their defensive tasks, they need to be strong **tacklers** and have the upper-body strength to wrestle the ball away from opponents. In attack both pace and good handling skills are very important.

At set pieces or breakdowns in play the pitch can be split into two rectangles through the play, parallel with and bounded by the touchlines. Quite simply, the larger segment is called the **open side** and the smaller is known as the **blind side** (or **narrow** or **short side**).

The flankers usually specialise so that one is always on the open side of the play (particularly at scrums) while the other takes responsibility for the blind side. The **open-side flanker's** main focus in defence is to nullify the threat posed by the opposing outside half. He will aim to do this by forcing his target into making an error, by tackling him in possession or by **charging down** his attempt to kick ahead. The **blind-side flanker** is more of a stopper

– one who occupies a blocking role in the event of a surprise attack down the narrower side of a scrum.

Sometimes, however, the flankers will operate on the left/right basis: that is, the same player occupies the left side of the scrum irrespective of whether it is on the open or blind side. Each flanker is usually tall and with good basketball skills that can be deployed at the line-out.

The **Number Eight** is the last forward in the scrum and for that reason is often known as the **back row**. Athleticism and speed are the main requisites for this position, which requires its occupant to be a jack of all the rugby player's trades and master of them all. They bring aerial power to the **tail** of the line-out, add shove to the scrum and add an extra dimension in attack and defence, employing the **pick-and-go** to launch drives from their own scrum possession and providing cover to the traditional drift defence when opponents have scrum possession.

The skills of the flanker and Number Eight are interchangeable and quite often in matches at the top level the flanker will be seen occupying the Number Eight's position (and vice versa) when the opposition have the feed at scrums.

What are substitutes and replacements?

A team nominates a pool of up to seven additional players to start the match as bench substitutes or replacements. There are usually four specialist forwards – a prop, a hooker, a second-row and a back-row forward – and three backs who provide cover for the scrum half, the outside half and the three-quarters or fullback.

Players can be substituted for any reason during a game, but once a substitution has been made it cannot be reversed (unless a front-row player becomes injured, in which case a substituted prop or hooker may return to the game). Replacements are used when a player is injured in the course of a match and cannot continue.

If, as the result of injuries or a sending off, a team is unable to field a front row then **uncontested** scrums take place. In effect the scrum becomes de-powered.

If an injured player needs only temporary treatment for a blood injury, he is allowed to go off to be patched up before returning.

A team can replace him with a temporary or **blood replacement** while the injury is treated in the **blood bin**.

So how are teams numbered?

Starting from the back and working forward, teams are universally numbered as follows:

THE BACKS
15	Fullback
14	Right wing three-quarter
13	Outside centre three-quarter (or centre in the South Pacific)
12	Inside centre three-quarter (or second five-eighth)
11	Left wing three-quarter
10	Outside half (or first five-eighth)
9	Scrum half (or halfback)

THE FORWARDS
8	Number Eight
7	Open-side flanker
6	Blind-side flanker
5	Right lock forward
4	Left lock forward
3	Tight-head prop
2	Hooker
1	Loose-head prop

SUBSTITUTES (usually)
16	Substitute hooker
17	Substitute prop
18	Substitute lock
19	Substitute back-row forward
20	Substitute scrum half
21	Substitute outside half
22	Substitute three-quarter/fullback

This number pattern is laid down by the IRB, though several players – for superstitious reasons, perhaps – have been known to flaunt the convention. The distinguished England outside centre Jeremy Guscott seemed to shun the No. 13 shirt and often appeared wearing the No. 12 shirt, while David Campese (Australia), Christophe Dominici (France) and more recently Shane Williams (Wales) all began their Test careers wearing the No. 11 shirt of the left wing. Later, however, when they were used by their nations as right wings, they retained their No. 11 jersey numbers, much to the confusion of journalists, commentators and spectators.

6.
Who Keeps Control of the Players?

Referees

The referee keeps control of the game on the pitch. He is the timekeeper and the official scorer though his main duty is to apply rugby's laws fairly and consistently during a match. It goes without saying that he must be neutral and maintain good communications with the players without being obtrusive.

Referees for international matches are appointed by the IRB. For other matches involving professional players the body organising their games will make the appointment. If a referee is injured during the course of a game a substitute official can replace him.

The tradition in rugby is that players do not argue with the referee's decision. For that reason it is the ideal sport for teenagers. The need for discipline in a physical contact sport is self-evident. Rugby involves frequent contact and the scope for thuggery is vast. Yet organised rugby enjoys an excellent reputation for restraining its physicality to the benefit of the game, and cheats or thugs are relatively rare.

Sanctions

From time to time, however, players do overstep the mark and have to accept punishment by the referee. There is a well-structured scale of sanctions available to officials to keep the offenders carefully in check.

Knock on

The referee punishes infringements according to their seriousness. Careless errors such as a **forward pass** or **knock-on** are typically punished by the award of a scrum feed against the side responsible for the error. The nature of the scrum formation is such that the side feeding the ball has a high likelihood of heeling it and using it to launch an attack. (If, as the result of a **charge-down** of a kick, the player defending the kick causes the ball to travel towards his opponent's goal line, play will continue: this is not a knock-on.)

More serious offences resulting in an unfair advantage for the offending team are punished by **free kicks** being awarded to the opposition. Free kicks enable teams to relieve pressure by kicking direct to touch from any part of the pitch. The non-kicking team then restarts the game by throwing in to a line-out at the place where the ball has crossed the touchline. Teams, however, are not compelled to kick for touch from a free kick. Alternatives include a **tap-and-go** or even an **up-and-under.**

The next disciplinary level is the award of a **penalty kick**. Here the non-offending team has the advantage of the throw-in if it chooses to kick into touch. Like scrums, line-outs are usually won by the side that throws in. If, however, the posts are within a kicker's range, the team may nominate a kick at goal and add three points to its score.

Free kicks and penalty kicks cannot be taken closer than 5 metres from the opponent's goal line. Most free kicks and penalty kicks are awarded for technical misdemeanours. Occasionally, however, referees have to intervene and award penalty kicks in the case of **obstruction** or foul play.

Obstruction includes deliberately forcing a way through team-mates who have heeled the ball from a scrum or recycled it from a ruck or maul. It also includes **shepherding**, where players attempt to shield team-mates carrying the ball, deliberately interfering with a player trying to get round a scrum after the ball has emerged from a put-in, or unfairly charging a player who is competing for possession of the ball. However, a player who runs for the ball shoulder to shoulder with an opponent is not committing an obstruction.

Foul play is defined as any action contrary to the spirit and letter of the laws. Foul play includes cheating, misconduct, punching, interfering with a player who does not have the ball, tripping, **dangerous play** (including deliberately collapsing a scrum, ruck or maul), gamesmanship, retaliation and persistent infringement. The **early tackle**, **late tackle** and charging or obstruction of a player who has kicked the ball is also an offence incurring a penalty under this heading.

Rugby's unique law

The referee's word is final and players must not argue once a decision has been made. It is a malaise of modern sport that **dissent** at referees' or umpires' decisions, usually in the form of **backchat**, is part and parcel of the game. Not Rugby Union! Players may politely enquire about a decision that a referee has made, but any form of dissent is punished by the **10-metre law**. Referees who feel their judgement is being challenged, or worse, undermined, will penalise teams that have already offended by marching them a further 10 metres closer to their own goal line. Clearly, if this occurs in the offending team's own half, their opponents will have an easier chance of collecting three points from a penalty kick at goal. This is a law that works well in rugby and seems to be unique to the game.

Cards, sin-bins and citings

In addition to the award of a penalty, the rugby referee may also caution the player responsible for foul play. The referee carries two cards that are produced to show that a player's actions warrant more severe punishment: the **yellow card** is used to temporarily expel a player from the pitch. The player sits out his punishment for a ten-minute cooling-off period in what is known as the **sin bin**. Once the punishment is served he is allowed to rejoin the game. If a player commits a very serious offence, the referee will show him the **red card**. This signifies that the player has been **sent off** and can take no further part in the game.

Sometimes players' dangerous actions are not seen by the referee or his **touch judges**. Even so, if unpunished foul play is suspected a team may **cite** an opponent, leading to an enquiry into the incident. Television footage, if available, may be used to ensure that a player is punished or exonerated.

As in the case of most red-card incidents, a player who is cited and found guilty of foul play will usually have to serve a period of suspension that prevents him from playing the game for a fixed period. The length of his suspension will depend on the seriousness of his case. Occasionally a player's offence might be so dangerous, or his past record so poor, that his Union might take the extremely rare action of banning him from the game for life.

The advantage law

Apart from keeping control of a physical game, referees are pivotal to the ebb and flow of a rugby match. Two particular laws need to be administered consistently in order to improve the game as a spectacle.

The **advantage law** is a unique rule to rugby. It permits referees to use wide discretion and delay whistling for an infringement if a clear territorial or tactical advantage accrues to the non-offending team. Its application requires imagination and experience. Referees who aspire to officiating at the top level will need a very good grasp of this concept. Effective application of the rule adds immensely to the pleasure of the game, for both players and spectators. There is no set time for which referees have to allow advantage to continue – it is up to their discretion. They are, however, encouraged to shout 'advantage over' for the benefit of the players when they feel the advantaged side has clearly benefited.

If the expected advantage is not gained, the referee must return to the **original offence** and award the non-offending team the scrum or penalty kick as appropriate. For this reason, experienced players will often be seen to make deliberate mistakes or take speculative drops at goal when the referee has announced that advantage is being played. If there is a high likelihood that a team's place-kicker will collect three points from a penalty kick awarded in a favourable position then it makes sense for the non-offending team to take the kick instead of gambling on a possible score arising.

Offside

Arguably the most important law that referees must police is **offside**. In general play, a player is offside if he is in front of a team-mate who has kicked, touched or is carrying the ball.

Even so, being in an offside position is not in itself an offence, unless it obstructs the attempts of the opposing side. For as long as the offside player does not interfere with play, does not play the ball or, if he is within 10 metres of an opponent who is waiting to play the ball, makes a positive attempt to retire to an onside position, he will not be penalised.

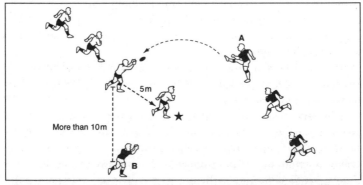

Offside. When A kicks, B is offside. Once catcher has advanced 5m to the starred position, B is played onside.

Players who are in an offside position but not within 10 metres of an opponent waiting to play the ball are played onside once the opponent taking possession of the ball has run 5 metres with it, has kicked it or has passed it, or has deliberately touched the ball (without necessarily catching it).

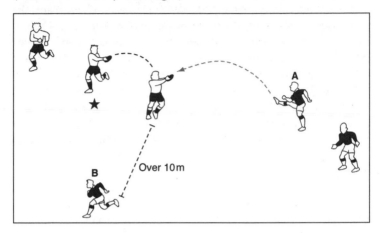

Over 10 m

Offside. When A kicks, B is offside. Once catcher passes to starred player, B is played onside.

Offside players can also be played onside by the actions of their team-mates. If a player is offside because a team-mate behind him has kicked the ball, then he is played onside if the kicker runs in front of him. That is why players who kick ahead in open play invariably follow their kicks. Moreover, if the offside player retreats from his position until he is behind any team-mate who has advanced from an onside position, he is automatically played onside.

If, at a kickoff or drop-out, a player drifts in front of the team-mate who takes the kick, then the referee will award a scrum feed to the non-infringing team.

Referees need to be alert to the phenomenon of **lazy running** in these circumstances. This is a cynical attempt (perfected by some of the world's top teams) to pretend to be retreating from an offside to an onside position, but at the same time managing to get in the path of a promising attack by the opposition and so destroying it.

At rucks, mauls and set pieces, all players not participating in them must stand behind an imaginary offside line. This is a line running the width of the pitch and through the back foot of the **hindmost** team-mate participating in a ruck, maul or scrum. The corresponding line at the line-out is drawn 10 metres back.

Strict application of the offside laws is necessary to give teams the space and confidence to make the game more free-flowing. There is nothing more annoying – for teams and spectators – than a referee who does not apply the letter of the law in this respect. Teams that sense refereeing weaknesses in the offside department succeed in suffocating enterprising back play and the game as a spectacle suffers.

Occasionally an offside player cannot avoid contact with the ball or a player carrying it and an **accidental offside** takes place. This type of infringement is punished by a scrum rather than a penalty kick, with the feed awarded to the non-offending side.

Safety first

Great onus is placed on referees to ensure the health and safety of players, particularly at scrums where there is great potential for serious injury. For this reason the IRB has recently issued referees with a new **engagement** code designed to stabilise scrums and reduce the occurrence of **collapses**. The IRB has also reminded its top referees that scrum-halves must feed the ball in straight, a simple law that is not always rigorously applied.

Spectators and television viewers will hear the referee call: 'Crouch-Touch-Pause-Engage' before the scrum half feeds. Ideally, the scrum feed is quickly made before one side has the chance to exert any pressure. If the heel is swiftly completed, the ball emerges from the tunnel at speed, ready for the next phase of play to be launched.

Rugby diehards say that the new sequence – it is the pause instruction which is the recent innovation – de-powers the scrum and makes striking for the ball uncompetitive. Even so, the early signs are that the law change has had its desired effect. Gone are the days when front rows comprising three 18-stone hulks smashed into each other with a force that could often be heard from the touchline. Even so, the number of collapses remains high and that must remain a worry for the law-makers.

There is a lesson from history here, too. Down the years major developments in the game have gone hand in hand with changes to its laws. The changes have always been intended to benefit the players and the game – making play safer and sometimes more open. Inevitably, however, coaches have concentrated on finding ways round the laws.

Ball touching the referee

The referee has the power to wave play on if the ball or a player carrying it touches him in the field of play, provided no advantage (or disadvantage) accrues to either team. If an advantage is gained then the referee will whistle for a scrum and award the feed to the side that last played the ball.

If a player carrying the ball in his own in-goal area touches the referee, a touchdown for a 22-metre drop-out will be awarded. If the player carrying the ball in his opponent's in-goal area touches the referee then a try is awarded.

When the ball touches the referee in the in-goal areas but is not in any player's possession, then the referee will award defenders the touchdown for the drop-out or attackers a try if, in the referee's opinion, it would otherwise have been gained.

What does the referee need to carry?

The referee carries a coin for the toss-up at the start of a match, red and yellow cards for use if a player is sent off or sin-binned, pencil and paper to keep the score, a stopwatch to keep time and a whistle to control play.

Touch judges

The officials who follow the play from the touchlines are called touch judges. Their prime duty is to raise their flag when the ball crosses the touchline, mark the place where a line-out takes place and point to the team that has the throw-in.

Touch judges keep their flags raised if the ball has been thrown in by the side not entitled to do so or if the thrower-in has stepped onto the field of play before feeding the line-out. His flag will also remain raised when, at a quick throw-in, the wrong ball is used or anyone other than the thrower has touched it. The only time a referee's decision can be altered on the field of play is when he has allowed play to continue without seeing that a touch judge has his flag raised to indicate that the ball has gone into touch, that a player carrying it has stepped in touch or the throw-in was invalid, or when he has seen an incident of foul play. The touch judge signals foul play by holding his flag horizontally and pointing it at right angles to the touchline. The referee may then take whatever action he deems necessary.

Line-out signal: touch judge points to team throwing in.

Foul play signal: touch judge points flag horizontally to alert referee.

Touch judges also stand behind the posts when goal attempts from conversions or penalty kicks are made. The touch judges raise their flags to indicate to the referee that a kick has been successful.

Rugby is a conservative game and developments often happen very slowly. For example, as long ago as March 1909 the IRB debated the appointment of neutral touch judges (for international matches). They even went a stage further, with notice of a motion being given by the Welsh representative on the Board that, where neutral touch judges are appointed it was desirable they shall report cases of rough, foul or unfair play as soon as possible to the referee. The notice was given that the matter should be discussed at the 1910 annual meeting.

Well, it was not until the 1980s that approval was finally given for neutral touch judges to be appointed at international level. Up until then touch judges were usually officials – members of the Union committee or former referees – from one of the participating teams, so a bit like Arsène Wenger and Sir Alex Ferguson running the lines when Arsenal and Manchester United have met in football's Premiership!

Nowadays, thank goodness, they are top-class referees, just in case the referee becomes injured and is required to retire, and often they come from the Nation that provides the referee. Their refereeing background and neutrality also justifies their interventions in the matter of foul play. So matters that were clearly identified as issues in the first decade of the twentieth century were finally addressed seventy years later.

Six rugby terms used in other languages

Apertura	Italian expression for the outside half – 'one who makes the openings'. The same word is used in Spanish.
Bachwr	The 'bach' gives it away – it's the Welsh translation for hooker.
Heelagter	Afrikaans (South African) for fullback.
Hors-jeu	Literally 'out of the game' – the French expression for offside.
Pot	New Zealand term for a drop at goal.
Talonneur	French for 'the heeler' – i.e., the hooker.

What's a TMO?

Referees at international and other levels of the professional game today are also assisted by a **TMO** – the television match official. They were first used in internationals in June 2000 after the Super 12 competitions had made good use of the innovation.

What is a loose-head?

The first international match in which a TMO was called on to adjudicate was the Test between New Zealand and Tonga at Albany in 2000. The All Blacks were already 55–0 ahead when Mark Hammett, their hooker, charged for the Tongan goal line from a line-out. He was held up, a maul developed and several bodies were seen to cross the line. The ball was buried beneath a mass of bodies, the English referee Steve Lander whistled and players, spectators and the television audience awaited his ruling.

Instead of making a decision, the referee gave a new signal. Outlining a rectangle with his hands as if taking part in a game of charades, he turned to the stands and, on his microphone, addressed a colleague sitting in an unseen television studio. He was heard to ask his helper: 'Have a look at that one, please.'

It was the first time that a referee had called for the backup of video evidence to form a decision regarding the validity of a test try. The TMO subsequently ruled in favour of the New Zealanders and the referee announced: 'Try, fellahs.'

At present the TMO can only be called upon to study video evidence regarding the scoring of tries. Referees are not yet entitled to refer to video replays to inform law decisions in other aspects of the game.

Six politicians who played rugby

Idi Amin	No, he didn't play for Scotland, but he did play rugby in his youth.
Jacques Chaban-Delmas	French Prime Minister who was capped once as a wing in 1945.
Bill Clinton	Played in college matches while on a Rhodes Scholarship to Oxford in the 1960s.
Ché Guevara	A promising flanker with the San Isidro club in Argentina in the 1950s.

Dick Spring	Well-known politician in the Irish Republic, who played fullback for Ireland in the 1970s.
Denis Thatcher	Well, he was married to a quite well-known politician! Denis was a London Society referee in the 1950s and touch-judged for England when they played France in Paris in 1956.

Is there an association that represents the interests of leading players?

Elite players' interests in England are represented by the Professional Rugby Players' Association (**PRA**). Rugby is a tough, physically demanding sport and the demands on players at the highest levels have become a cause for concern. Issues such as the number of games played and burnout are near the top of the PRA's agenda for the wellbeing of their members.

The Association is also aiming to get its voice heard in an important debate that is taking place between the RFU (Rugby Football Union) and the Premiership clubs over how the elite players are managed. The necessity for this debate has arisen as the result of a longstanding club v country argument over the release of players from their clubs for international match commitments. It is a debate that has already taken place among the French elite but is not a problem in the Tri-Nations, where players in international squads are centrally contracted to their national Unions.

7.
What About Tactics?

What exactly are tactics?

Rugby matches comprise a succession of passages of play, called **phases**. The passages are punctuated either informally by **rucks** and mauls when play breaks down because a player has been held or tackled, or by formal restarts through penalty kicks, free kicks, scrums and line-outs when the referee whistles for an infringement or the ball goes into touch.

The team that feeds a scrum or throws in at a line-out usually expects to win possession. Similarly, when play breaks down the team whose player is tackled or held expects to recycle possession at the ensuing ruck or maul. This means that teams know when the ball should be coming their way and their players – usually those in the back division – can plan in advance how they will use this possession. Their plans are called **tactics**.

Ultimately tactics are designed to yield points through scoring actions. Traditionally teams achieve points by moving forward towards their opponent's goal line in order to put themselves into a position from which scores might follow. Invariably the process of moving forward depends on having possession and retaining it.

What is open play?

Open play is the name given to most aspects of the game where the ball is moving faster than the players. It is usually the most attractive part of a rugby match to watch, especially for a newcomer to the game. As a rule of thumb, the longer the phases last (and therefore the fewer interruptions and stoppages enforced by the referee), the more open the game is.

Running and passing

The underlying principle of open rugby is to move the ball into space. For that reason teams that set out to play the open game aim to use their possession for passing movements that transfer the ball quickly to a player who has sufficient room to make a break through the opposition's defence.

Passes are usually aimed to be caught between the waist and chest, and ideally should be directed in front of the receiver so that he accelerates onto the ball. The game should be played going forward at speed – that way defenders are under pressure to reorganise their lines, giving the team in possession the opportunity of exploiting gaps.

The first target for the team in possession is to breach the so-called **advantage line**. This means that when the ball emerges from a scrum, line-out, ruck or maul the team in possession aims to carry it beyond an imaginary line that runs the width of the pitch through the middle of the set piece or breakdown point. Once a team's player has carried the ball beyond this line territory has been gained, placing the team closer to its focus, the opposition goal line.

Teams usually achieve this aim through running or passing the ball to a player who, by riding a tackle, changing pace, **swerving**, **sidestepping,** working a **scissors** move or **dummying** manages to penetrate the defence. Once the defence is breached the player heads for the goal line or seeks support from his team-mates so the attack can be continued.

Sometimes the aim is achieved by playing the **wide game**. Quick passing away from the set piece or breakdown is designed to spread the ball out to the wings and stretch the opposition's defence. A stretched defence means that the player carrying the ball has more room in which to manoeuvre and use his speed to break the advantage line.

Kicking

When teams are in possession the tactics used to make ground often include kicking. One of the backs – usually the outside half, but sometimes the scrum half or even the inside centre – will assume responsibility for making this decision and choosing the type of kick to be used.

When kicking is used as an attacking tactic in open play the kicks are usually **punts** – the kicker dropping the ball from his hands and striking it with his foot before it lands on the ground. The punt will usually be one of several types.

The up-and-under is invariably launched from the area between the two 10-metre lines. Its purpose is to put pressure on the opposition defence – in particular the **back-three** comprising the wings and fullback. The kicking side will hope for two outcomes from a well-judged punt of this type: the falling trajectory of a high steepling kick will be difficult to judge and will be dropped; and the time the ball is in the air will give the kicker's team-mates the opportunity to **follow up** and arrive as the ball comes to ground. If the opposition muff their catch then the followers-up have the chance to regain possession and press home an attack that might lead to a score.

The **cross-field** kick to the touchline is a variation on the up-and-under. The aim is for the player on the kicker's team to jump for the ball as it lands near or over the opposition's goal line and flop over for a try. It is a kick that takes great precision to master and was successfully employed by Jonny Wilkinson during England's memorable Rugby World Cup triumph in Australia in 2003.

The **chip kick** is a short punt ahead that either the kicker or one of his colleagues hopes to run onto and catch before it bounces on the ground. Useful from anywhere from the halfway line to the opposition's twenty-two, the point of the kick is to make advancing defenders stop in their tracks and turn back to cover any danger. The kicker will expect to take advantage of the temporary pause while defenders turn through 180 degrees and overtake them in the race for the ball.

A less predictable variation on this theme but one that has the same objective is the **grubber kick.** Here the punt is deliberately aimed towards the ground but, because of the difficulty of predicting which way a rugby ball will bounce, the chances of the tactic paying off are less certain. Even so, the objective once again is to turn the defence, enabling the kicker or a team-mate to overtake and hopefully gather the bouncing ball before racing clear to continue the attack or score. It's also a useful kick to use when finding touch outside the 22-metre lines.

Less common nowadays are two favourite tactical kicks from the past. The **cross kick** was a punt performed usually by wings who had just managed to wriggle outside an opponent. Sensing, perhaps, that there was insufficient space to run clear, the wing would then punt the ball across the pitch from near the touchline. Team-mates were expected to follow up down the middle of the field in the expectation of gathering the cross kick and running in for a score.

The best modern example of this type of score was the try by Philippe Saint-André for France in the Grand Slam showdown with England at Twickenham in 1991. On that occasion the audacious French launched an attack from their dead-ball line no less, continued it with a couple of chip kicks along the right touchline before Didier Camberabero, their outside half, cross-kicked from inside the English half. There, unmarked after taking a path along the middle of the field, was Saint-André, who gathered the ball to score a picture-book try under the English posts. For all that, though, the cross kick as an attacking move is relatively rare today.

So, too, is the **box kick** that was such an integral part of Welsh scrum half play in the 1960s and 1970s when Clive Rowlands and Gareth Edwards were in their heyday. Best launched 15 to 20 metres from the touchline and from the no-man's-land between halfway and the opposition's twenty-two, the scrum half aims to hook his punt over his shoulder towards the touchline so that it lands inside the twenty-two, where his blind-side wing or a back-row forward run on to gather the ball and continue the attack.

Six occasions when the weather disrupted rugby

1885 Heavy rain flooded the pitch at Ormeau in Belfast during the Ireland–Scotland fixture. The match was called off after thirty minutes and a replay was arranged.

1908 The England–Wales match at Bristol was a complete mystery to the 25,000 spectators, referee and most of the players on the pitch. It was played in dense fog.

1913 Weather conditions were so severe during the New Zealand–Australia Test in windy Wellington that the referee, taking pity on the players, split the game into four quarters rather than the customary two halves.

1925 Bad light hampered play in the second half of the Scotland–France international at the Inverleith ground in Edinburgh during an eclipse of the sun.

1927 Driving rain and an icy wind caused havoc among the players in the Ireland–Scotland match in Dublin. So severe were the conditions that one of the Irish team was treated for hypothermia.

1991 The match between the USA and France in Colorado Springs kicked off in a downpour that developed into a severe electric storm. The match was abandoned before half-time.

How is the tight game played?

The **tight game** is an alternative means for teams to move forward and at the same time retain possession. Tight play is characterised by phases of play that predominately feature scrums, line-outs, rucks and mauls, aspects of the game designed to test the skills of the forwards. A team that adopts a tight game as its tactics therefore expects to play to its forwards and depends on them to win the ball, take it forward and recycle it before launching another phase of play – usually another passage of play that features rucking and mauling.

Scrums and line-outs

Scrums and line-outs are rich starting points for teams adopting the tight game. Possession is usually retained by the side that feeds the set piece. Teams can therefore plan their tight moves off scrums and line-outs.

At scrums the tight game is usually launched by a Number Eight picking the ball up as it is heeled back but before it emerges to the backs. He will then typically charge forward to engage the opposition until he is smothered in a maul that sucks in forwards from both the opposition and his own team. His own forwards will aim to use their upper-body strength to help maul the ball back through their hands in order for another forward or the scrum half to launch the next attack.

The point of drawing opponents into the maul is to create space elsewhere on the pitch so that when the ball is recycled the scrum half can spin it out to his backs who can adopt the open game to take advantage of any gaps or weaknesses in the defence caused by drawing defenders into the maul.

Sometimes the forwards adopt a tight formation at the back of a maul that enables them to roll off the back of it once they have secured possession and move forward in a very close formation, churning from maul to maul to make ground and find a gap in the defence. The move is very difficult to defend and the closeness of the forwards reduces the risks of handling errors when the ball is moved from forward to forward. Clearly, when this is done skilfully near the opposition's goal line there is a strong chance of scoring a try.

If the Number Eight's drive ends with a tackle then the ball will be released on the ground and the forwards from both teams will converge on it to form a ruck. Players are not allowed to handle the ball in a ruck until it emerges, so the next phase of action will usually be launched by the scrum half. The principle, however, remains the same for rucks as for mauls: draw in as many opponents as possible to create space away from the breakdown.

The line-out offers a different set of tight options. With both packs spread out between the narrow confines of the 5-metre and 15-metre lines, there is ample scope for a catcher at the tail of the line-out to drive forward and suck opponents in at a breakdown and recycle the ball. Typically a Number Eight or one of the flankers will launch the move from the back. Then the front-row or second-row forwards who have **peeled off** from the front of the line-out at the moment the ball has been thrown in come round the tail to support the ball-carrier as he commits defenders to the tackle. The ruck or maul is formed and the side that has taken the ball forward should regain possession.

Rucking and mauling

The rucks and mauls are less formal than scrums and line-outs but serve the same function: to restart a match after a breakdown. Whereas referees have to whistle before a scrum or line-out takes place, rucks and mauls are ways in which teams use their own initiative to continue play after it has broken down through a tackle or spilled pass.

The essential difference between a ruck and a maul is that the ball is on the ground in the former but retained in the hands in the latter. Players must not handle the ball in a ruck.

The start of a ruck

At both ruck and maul participants must remain on their feet and bound to their team-mates. The punishment for transgressing or deliberately **collapsing** is a penalty kick awarded to the non-offending team.

The start of a maul

Effective rucking depends on similar skills to scrummaging: the players are bound in and aim to heel the ball back along the ground to their scrum half. Unlike the scrum, however, forwards do not have fixed positions in a ruck, which means that its shape frequently changes. This informality can lead to difficulties if the ruck is not properly policed by an observant referee.

To maintain the dynamic of the ruck the law-makers have ruled that players joining it must come **through-the-gate**. The expression means that players must add themselves to the formation only by joining it from behind the hindmost foot of a team-mate who is already bound into the ruck. There is a similar restriction on players joining the maul, which has a similar informal structure to the ruck except that the ball is in the players' hands rather than on the ground.

At ruck and maul the loose player must join from behind his team's offside line

Teams taking the ball into the maul or setting up the ruck are expected to recycle it. The chances of retaining possession in these circumstances, however, are not so high as at the set pieces, and rucks and mauls are often the scenes of turnovers.

Play often breaks down irretrievably at rucks. On such occasions the referee will blow his whistle and order a scrum to restart the game. The team that had been going forward takes the **put-in**.

For that reason rucks are a safer bet for retaining possession when the ball is not clearly recycled from them. The side taking the ball into the ruck usually has the initial impetus. The impulse the ruck is given usually results in the side in possession moving forward so, if the ball does not emerge, the referee will award them the scrum put-in.

In mauls, however, the team in possession has to **use it or lose it**. Teams will aim to recycle possession by working the ball back to the scrum half by hand, or convert the maul into a **driving maul** or **rolling maul** to maintain forward momentum. If the maul makes no progress it becomes a **static maul** and the referee will blow his whistle and award the ensuing scrum put-in to the side without the ball.

When forwards realise that the maul is heading for the static state, they will invariably try to convert it into a ruck by putting the ball on the ground, thereby improving their chances of retaining possession, should play break down.

How do teams defend?

It is often said that attack is the best form of defence and most teams will adopt this as a tactic, in which case the situations outlined above are likely to develop. Attacking defence is most likely to be seen when a match is in its dying stages and the team's chance of winning or saving it depends on a last-ditch break-out from a defensive position deep inside its own half. Otherwise, a team might use the tactic for its surprise element. The least likely move expected of a defending team is an attacking one. Quite often when attack from defence is successful it leads to spectacular tries that involve long, flowing moves extending the length of the pitch.

On most occasions, however, sides under pressure will adopt defensive tactics with the immediate aim of averting danger near their own line and making headway towards the halfway line. Sides usually adopt the drift defence or **blitz defence** to avert the threat of a break or score by their opponents.

The drift defence is a deliberate attempt to shepherd the attacking side across the field into a cul-de-sac near the touchline, thereby closing down the space available for attack and forcing the team in possession to set up a ruck or maul in order to recycle the ball.

The blitz defence, by contrast, is an aggressive advance by the defending side. The aim is to close down the space in the no-man's-land between the opposing backs, forcing the ball-carriers into making hurried decisions that often result in errors and breakdowns in play. It is a method that South Africa has occasionally employed to good effect to ruffle the All Blacks, while closer to home it has been a successful tactic of the London Wasps at English club level.

Six films/plays featuring Rugby Union

A Run for Your Money   Classic Ealing comedy (1949) starring Alec Guinness, Moira Lister, Hugh Griffith and Joyce Grenfell. The story centres on the adventures of a pair of Welsh rugby supporters up in London for the England–Wales Twickenham rugby weekend.

Grand Slam   Feature-length comedy play from BBC Wales (first aired in 1978) about a Welsh club's boozy trip to Paris for the 1977 France–Wales encounter. Windsor Davies reprises his Sergeant-Major Williams' accent from *It Ain't Half Hot, Mum* and the rheumy-eyed Hugh Griffith again features in a cameo role, this time as the senior-citizen Welshman abroad for a rugby weekend.

Alone it Stands   John Breen's play is a tribute to the Munster team that, in October 1978, beat the famous All Blacks 12–0: still the only time that New Zealand have lost on Irish soil. It recreates the wonderful atmosphere of Thomond Park in Limerick, where the game was played. First performed at Waterpark RFC in the west of Ireland in 1999, it became a West End hit in 2002 and was later successfully staged in Australia.

Alive 1992 film directed by Frank Marshall and adapted from Piers Paul Read's true story. Ethan Hawke stars in this tale of the fight for survival by members of the Old Christians RFC from Montevideo after their charter plane crash-lands in the Andes en route to a match in Santiago, Chile.

Le Placard (The Closet) Daniel Auteuil and Gérard Depardieu are the leads in this 2001 politically incorrect French farce set in a condom factory! Depardieu caricatures French forwards in his role as coach of the works rugby team.

The One With All The Rugby Episode first aired in 1998 from the long-running American sitcom, *Friends*. Ross, dating Emily, an English woman, is overcome by a fit of bravado and takes up the challenge to play in a game of rugby from a group of her friends visiting from home. Former Cambridge rugby blue Mark Thomas makes a guest appearance.

Tackling

This is the most obvious way in which individual defenders snuff out dangerous attacks. The tackler must approach the player with the ball and aim to wrap his arms around the carrier's body somewhere between the shoulders and the ankle. The trick, then, is for the tackler to use his momentum to bring his target to the ground, at the same time maintaining his hold on the ball-carrier.

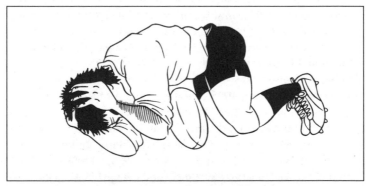

Tackle area. The player must release the ball.

The area surrounding a tackle is often untidy and this aspect of the game is policed very strictly by referees. The tackled player must immediately pass the ball or release it. In releasing, the tackled player is permitted to place the ball on the ground or push it along the ground (though not forward), but he must do so without delay. If he does not, then he will be penalised and automatically lose possession. Likewise, if an opponent wilfully dives on the tackled player so as to deliberately prevent an immediate release, the penalty will be awarded to the tackled player's team.

After a tackle has taken place, any other player who intends to use the ball must be on his feet when he plays the ball. Once the release has taken place, players converging on the tackled player or the ball might set up a ruck or maul. Or, if the players from the tackler's team are first to the breakdown, they might win a turnover and the threat from the opposition is averted.

Tackle area penalty. The next player to touch the ball must be on his feet.

When a tackle takes place near the goal line a try will be awarded to a tackled player if his momentum carries him over his opponents' line and he touches the ball down behind it.

Players practise the standard tackle in training using tackle bags – large stuffed kitbags that enable the tackler to perfect his technique. The most effective tackle will be carried out at speed, the tackler driving his body at his target. The head of the tackler is angled away from the side of his target (so the tackler does not find his head trapped between the tackled player's body and the ground), and the arms are locked around the tackled player's body.

Tackling brings out the courage in players. The player built like a pocket battleship will **crash-tackle** his opponents out of a game; the slender, artful one will use his balance and the skill of a judo black-belt to arrest his target and cause him to fall. In between there is the aptly named 'toilet' tackle. The tackler crouches, sits, waits and hopes that the ball-carrier will run into him and topple over – not a recommended approach.

More Kicking

Line kicking is the main form of defence for sides who have gained possession. One of the **midfield backs** – usually the outside half or inside centre – will aim to boot the ball into touch near the halfway line in order to relieve the pressure on their forwards.

The classic line kick is the **torpedo** punt. The kicker cuts the instep of his foot across the longer axis of the ball as it leaves his hands, so that a spin is imparted to its trajectory. At first the ball spirals away from the touchline and the kicker before reaching its highest point. Then, as it goes into a tailspin, the ball spirals back towards the touchline and out of play. The finest kickers will gain for their sides the best part of 50 to 60 metres by this method of defence – just the fillip a pack needs.

Is there a master plan?

Tactics, of course, will vary, but all rugby matches follow a pattern of play.

A match is started through a kickoff. Thereafter players catch or pick up the ball and run with it. In the course of their runs they will pass, throw or kick the ball. Players belonging to the side not in possession will tackle, push or charge opponents to prevent their progress. When play breaks down, the game restarts – either through a scrum or line-out, or if the ball is not dead, through a ruck or maul. The ultimate plan is to score a try or to force points through penalty goals or dropped goals.

Martin Johnson, the successful England Rugby World Cup captain, has always seen rugby at the highest level as a simple game – if basics such as passing, kicking, tackling, running with the ball and maintaining discipline are correctly mastered, everything else follows.

Six unusual rugby matches

1873   Oxford forward George Podmore was bitten by a stray dog during the Varsity match.

1892   The famous Barbarians rugby club was beaten *at rugby* by its soccer counterparts, the Corinthians football club.

1909   At Carmarthen, a team of Williams brothers beat a team of Randall brothers in a seven-a-side match.

1950   The first recorded instance of a father playing against his son in a first-class match. George Nepia senior and junior were opposing fullbacks in a match staged in Gisborne, New Zealand.

1957   When Bush met Wanganui in New Zealand, three referees were needed before the final whistle.

1974   Actresses drew 10–10 against a team of models in a well-attended charity match staged at Sunbury-on-Thames.

8.

Everyone Knows Jonny Wilkinson, But Who Was Alex Obolensky?

Jonny Wilkinson

Jonny Wilkinson was the England player who above all typified the professionalism and determination of the 2003 Grand Slam and World Cup-winning side.

Arguably the finest all-round outside half in world rugby, he was already known as a deadly accurate place-kicker whose name dominated the International Championship's book of records – most points by a player in a Championship season (89 in 2001), holder of the individual match record with 35 points against Italy the same year, and the leading points scorer in the history of English Test rugby, overtaking his Newcastle boss and mentor, Rob Andrew.

But it was Wilkinson's readiness to put his body on the line that overshadowed all his brilliant kicking and tactical direction in England's *annus mirabilis* in 2003. Outside-halves down the years have not exactly been renowned for their bravery in defence. Yet in match after match in the Championship and World Cup he put in the kind of big-hitting tackles that demoralise opponents and inspire forwards. Simon Barnes, sports columnist of *The Times*, wrote after that year's

Grand Slam match in Dublin: 'You wondered if Wilkinson wore a No. 10 on his back to show how many of him there were on the pitch. Head on, at full speed from behind, fast men, big men – it all came as one. With perfect technique he slammed them all to the ground. He knocked the stuffing out of them.'

Wilkinson won the first of his **caps** at the age of 18 years, 314 days as a replacement wing for Mike Catt against Ireland in 1998, making him the youngest England cap since 1927. He spent a season playing at centre before becoming England's first-choice at outside half for the World Cup in 1999.

But after getting his World Cup winners' medal in 2003 there followed four years of unparalleled disaster as injury after injury sidelined him from top-class rugby. He made a cameo appearance in 2005 for the ill-fated Lions in New Zealand before eventually returning to resume normal service and set alight the Six Nations in 2007 after England had passed through a rough patch of eight defeats in nine matches the previous year. Jonny immediately steered England back to winning ways and restored winning hopes to the Red Rose's army of dedicated supporters.

Prince Alex Obolensky

Alex Obolensky, an exiled Russian prince studying at Oxford University, set no special records for England. Indeed he only appeared four times in the white jersey with red rose. Yet his deeds against the All Blacks on a cold January day in 1936 made him a household name even before the television age.

His two tries against New Zealand on his debut made 'Obo' an overnight star. He was an electric runner who used his acceleration to deceive opponents, but it was his love of the unorthodox that marked him out from the run-of-the-mill wings of the day. His second try against the All Blacks, in particular, was a classic. Receiving the ball far out on his right wing, he ghosted through the New Zealand defence to finish off scoring wide out to the left of the posts.

Captured on film by Movietone News, it was probably the first famous try to be seen by a broad audience. Vivian Jenkins, the Welsh fullback at the time, recalled that he spent several hours at an Oxford Street cinema specially to see the two or three minutes of newsreel between feature films, so he could size up the Obolensky threat – Wales were due to play England a fortnight later.

Obolensky's fame has never waned, though he would never again set the rugby world alight. He kept his place for the three Championship matches in 1936 – a scoreless draw with Wales, defeat in Dublin and a one-point win against Scotland back at Twickenham, which was his last appearance in a cap match. He was killed tragically young in a flying accident early in World War II.

Who are the other famous names in Rugby Union?

Martin Johnson

Martin Johnson is the only Brit who has lifted the Rugby World Cup as a captain. England's most-capped lock, he overtook the record of Wade Dooley, the man he replaced at late notice to make his Test debut against France in 1993. For strength of character and sheer physical power, it is doubtful whether English rugby will find his like again.

Johnson quickly became a fixture in the England packs under the management of first Geoff Cooke and then Jack Rowell, forming with Martin Bayfield the engine room of the pack that laid the foundations of the 1995 Grand Slam. Strong and imperturbable, Johnson was the solid backbone of the scrum and an effective rucker and mauler who revelled in the frolics of the loose.

In 1997 he led the Lions to a series victory in South Africa, but it wasn't until Lawrence Dallaglio lost the captaincy in the spring of 1999 that Johnson became England's regular captain in the field.

He led his country to eight consecutive wins in 2000–1, but his absence from the Grand Slam showdown in Dublin in 2001 was the telling factor in England's abject defeat. The same summer he became the first player in modern times to captain the Lions on two tours, leading the side in a losing series in Australia.

Johnson's finest hours were still to come. In Dublin in 2003, England finally clinched the Six Nations Grand Slam before going on to achieve the sport's Holy Grail, winning the World Cup in Australia.

Where are they now? Six of England's World Cup winners

Neil Back Retired a year after the World Cup, but was persuaded by Clive Woodward to make one last stand: with the Lions in New Zealand in 2005. Now coaching back at his beloved Leicester Tigers club.

Matt Dawson The scrum half retired from rugby in 2006 before making a seamless transition to radio and television.

Martin Johnson Retired immediately after the Rugby World Cup in 2003. Went on a marathon world tour in his benefit year and, apart from working the after-dinner speaking circuit, is an indefatigable worker for charity.

Josh Lewsey The only member of the World Cup team to keep a regular place in the side after the final. Lewsey played twenty successive Tests before losing form in 2006. Still a force to be reckoned with – either playing for Wasps or England.

Steve Thompson Found it difficult to retain his zest for the game after the World Cup, and considered jacking in the professional game to join the police. Forced to retire on medical advice in 2007 after suffering a series of neck injuries.

Jonny Wilkinson The man who kicked the World Cup-winning goal had three years of almost constant injury. He finally returned to the England side in February 2007, having missed thirty England matches since the famous final.

Gareth Edwards

'The best rugby player in the world' was how Gareth Edwards was described in the 1970s. And when *Rugby World* magazine, the game's leading periodical, conducted a grass-roots poll to find the world's most famous rugby player, Edwards was the outright winner. He played in 53 successive Tests for Wales between 1967 and 1978, a record that spoke volumes for his strength and resilience, and during his career Wales won three Grand Slams, five Triple Crowns, five outright Five Nations Championships and two shared titles.

The assault on his Test match Everest began in 1967 as a teenager in Paris and he established base camp the next season when he began his fruitful partnership with Barry John. 'You throw them and I'll catch them,' was John's comment on the slightly wayward Edwards' service when they first met. But the scrum half worked to improve his passing and in 1969 was a key member of the Wales team that won the Triple Crown.

After a marvellous season in 1971 that included a Welsh Grand Slam and a first Lions Test series victory in New Zealand, Edwards finally scaled the heights when Barry John retired in 1972.

He stayed there for six outstandingly successful seasons, including a summer in South Africa in 1974 with an unbeaten Lions touring side. Assuming the mantle of tactical controller, Edwards was the linchpin in a Welsh side that lost only five times in 24 Five Nations matches. When he finally stood down in 1978, he held the record for most career tries for Wales (twenty), having earlier in his career become Wales's youngest-ever Test captain (aged 20). He later became a well-known television personality and was for many years one of the resident captains on the BBC's long-running *Question of Sport* quiz.

Mike Gibson

The late John Reason, rugby's shrewdest critic of the period between 1960 and 1990, rated Mike Gibson the greatest rugby player of his time.

Gibson filled the lead part for Ireland and the Lions in one of the longest-running shows in Test rugby. His classical qualities brought massive audiences to watch him perform either at outside half or centre for an unprecedented sixteen seasons on the highest stage.

The splendid vision he had in reading play, as well as his speed off the mark and sparkling sidestepping runs, gave an edge to Ireland's back line and a vintage Gibson performance was always worth travelling many miles to see. But it was with the 1971 Lions in New Zealand that his gifts reaped maximum rewards. His talents in defence and perception in attack were a key part of the only Lions Test series win against the All Blacks to date.

It was on that tour that he really blossomed as a centre, the majority of his Ireland caps up till then having been won playing in the outside-half jersey. The uncluttered view of the game he had from the middle of the three-quarter line gave him more scope to study lines of attack, and increased his own freedom to choose his options.

He called time on his rugby career in 1979, having become the world's most-capped player and after travelling on five Lions tours. Since his retirement no British or Irish back has come close to the quiet Ulsterman's claim to the title of best all-round post-war footballer in the Home Unions.

Jason Leonard

After England hooker Brian Moore had stood shoulder to shoulder with his new loose-head prop Jason Leonard for eighty minutes in Buenos Aires in 1990, he said: 'It was patently obvious that he's going to be an outstanding player.'

Leonard was, at 21, the youngest prop to play for England for twenty-seven years. Yet even in those relatively carefree days at the start of the 1990s, when players enjoyed a few beers after a match and went back on Monday mornings to their jobs outside rugby, it was clear that England had found a genuine grafter who would take some moving in the front row. He went on to become the first Englishman to win one hundred caps for his country and is the world's most-capped forward.

His dedication to training and fitness, and his discipline in adhering to the strict dietary regimen that are all part and parcel of the professional era enabled Leonard to stay at the top of his game during a decade that saw the demands on leading players change beyond all recognition. Throughout it all, moreover, he was the one constant in England's equation. Four times he featured in Grand Slam sides (1991, 1992, 1995 and 2003) and he was a member of England's 2003 Rugby World Cup-winning team.

Lawrence Dallaglio

It was the constructive and forthright play that he brought to England's 1993 Rugby World Cup Sevens triumph that catapulted Lawrence Dallaglio into the rugby limelight. Having almost achieved a full set of England representative honours as a youth, he subsequently broke into the England squad after the 1995 Rugby World Cup.

He proved such an outstanding loose forward that he quickly became the player England could not afford to drop. After Phil de Glanville relinquished his brief hold on the captaincy in succession to Will Carling, Dallaglio was given the skipper's armband when Clive Woodward entered the scene as head coach in November 1997. Dallaglio went on to lead his country only fourteen times. The victim of a tabloid sting in the spring of 1999, he was stripped of the captaincy and Martin Johnson took over for the summer Test against Australia.

During Dallaglio's time at the helm England enjoyed a Triple Crown season in 1998 and later the same year brought to an end South Africa's world record-equalling run of seventeen successive Test victories.

A long-term shoulder injury and a knee injury that brought a premature end to his Lions tour in Australia in 2001 disrupted his progress. But in 2003, after starting the Championship campaign on the bench against France, he found new reserves of strength and determination to reclaim his place alongside Neil Back and Richard Hill in a back row that has played together more times at Test level than any other international trio. Dallaglio showed he was back to his best in Dublin, where he scored the opening try of the winner-takes-all Grand Slam showdown with Ireland. Then, at the end of the year, he was an ever-present in England's successful assault on the Rugby World Cup in Australia – being on the field for the full 560 minutes of England's seven matches through to the end of the famous final.

Six rugby-loving lords

Lord Addington Lib-Dem peer who captains the Commons & Lords rugby team and has participated in two Parliamentary World Cup tournaments.

Lord Bannerman Johnnie Bannerman was Wakefield's Scottish counterpart in almost every respect. He won a then record thirty-seven caps in the 1920s and was later a president of the Scottish Rugby Union.

Lord Bledisloe In 1931, as Governor General of New Zealand, he presented a rugby trophy to foster rugby relations between his country and Australia. The Cup is the prize that the All Blacks and Wallabies play for to this day.

Lord Monro Langholm and Scotland's greatest rugby supporter was the late Hector Monro. He was a president of the Scottish Rugby Union.

Lord Rennell As Tremayne Rodd, the late Lord Rennell was Scotland's regular scrum half between 1958 and 1965. He played the game well into his sixties and organised the Houses of Parliament rugby team.

Lord Wakefield As Wavell Wakefield he was the most famous British rugby player of his generation. He held the record (thirty-one) for most international caps for England from the 1920s until 1969 and was later a prominent administrator and politician. His typically English character, undying love for the game and the pre-match Twickenham atmosphere are summarised in the immortal phrase: 'Champers at Twickers with Wakers.'

Mervyn Davies

Lean almost to the point of being skinny, Mervyn Davies dominated the back of the Welsh scrum and line-out in thirty-eight successive appearances between 1969 and 1976. An ever-present in the winning Lions Test series of 1971 (in New Zealand) and 1974 (in South Africa), he ended his career as the world's most-capped international in his position. He was a thoroughbred Number Eight at a time when the position was often occupied by converted locks or makeshift flankers.

Davies did not need his trademark jet-black hair tightly wrapped in a white sweatband to catch attention on the field. He played by instinct at a time when other Number Eights played by numbers. He had an uncanny sense of anticipation in loose play and with the ball in his hand displayed all the dextrous skills of a top-class basketball player. In defence he cut his opponents down with uncompromising tackles.

His entry to the Welsh side in 1969 coincided with the start of a long period of Welsh domination of the Five Nations Championship. Davies featured in two Grand Slam and three Triple Crown sides and captained a new-look Wales side in 1975 (Championship title) and 1976 (Grand Slam).

Captaincy brought to light hitherto unknown aspects of his character. His confidence as a player increased and his tactical reading of games was close to infallible. Wales lost only once in nine outings under his leadership before he suffered a brain haemorrhage while playing for Swansea in a cup match. Although he made a good recovery, his rugby career was abruptly cut off in its prime.

Will Carling

The public face of the English rugby successes between 1988 and 1996 undoubtedly belonged to its long-serving captain, Will Carling.

It was his polished three-quarter play that propelled him into an England side that was given little chance of beating France in Paris in 1988. Yet new manager Geoff Cooke's young bloods went down by only a point and Carling held his place in a Five Nations season of mixed fortunes, sharpening his defensive qualities and acclimatising to the extra pace of Test rugby.

By the end of the year, having established himself as a world-class player with a flair for the outside break, he was installed as captain, becoming the youngest man for fifty-seven years to hold the honour for England. He led the side to a 28–19 victory against Australia and never looked back after that.

A psychology student, Carling did not follow the tub-thumping school of leadership. Instead he worked closely, first with Geoff Cooke and later Jack Rowell, to engender in his sides a collective responsibility to adhere to game plans worked out at squad training. A purposeful atmosphere developed around a side that went on to claim four Triple Crowns, three Grand Slams and reached the World Cup final in 1991 and the semifinal four years later.

Carling's final record read fourty-four wins from fifty-nine matches as captain. There can be no better testimony to the effectiveness of his approach.

Willie-John McBride

Willie-John McBride was the forward who dominated northern hemisphere rugby when he was at his peak between 1966 and 1974. The Irishman was never found to be anything but the solid backbone of the scrum, both for his country and the Lions.

He was the first player to tour five times with the Lions and first showed his leadership potential with the successful class of 1971 in New Zealand, where he emerged as their pack leader. McBride had the respect of his colleagues – a leader whose followers genuinely warmed to his calm control and huge confidence.

He was the natural choice as skipper of the 1974 Lions, going on to inspire his team to complete an unbeaten tour of South Africa. The side won the Test series 3–0 against the Springboks, drawing the final match. No British/Irish side of the modern era realised anywhere near such a remarkable achievement.

Immense strength and fitness were the hallmarks of his play. As rucking and mauling became the vogue in rugby in the 1960s, so he applied his strength to the task of winning vital second-phase possession. His legs pumped like pistons to supply drive at the heart of rucks, and he used his mighty arms to prise the ball free in mauls. Then, as the demand for running, handling forwards increased, he even showed that he could join in the frolics of open play with the best of the pack.

For strength of character and sheer physical power, the only player who has come anywhere near to matching his standing was England's Martin Johnson. McBride was that good.

J P R Williams

When the International Board changed the law relating to **direct kicking to touch** in 1968, J P R Williams was the first of a new breed of fullback to effectively exploit the new attacking opportunities offered. He went on to become the master of the fullback incursion to the three-quarter line, made the position in the Welsh side his own for a decade and eventually retired from the Test side in 1981 as his country's leading cap winner.

Apart from his flair in attack, he was remembered for his rock-solid defence, the first requisite of a fullback. He thrived on making blockbusting tackles, and when the ball was in the air it seemed to be attracted magnet-like to his bread-basket arms. He never flinched and rarely misfielded. Indeed, he so enjoyed the contact nature of rugby football that, when injuries dictated, he once started a tour Test for Wales in Australia as a flanker.

Williams was easily recognised on the field. For most of his career he wore his hair fashionably long, but it was the socks rolled down to the ankles that conveyed the impression that he was ready for the physical contact he so clearly relished.

Williams left his admirers in Wales a host of happy memories. His indestructible spirit helped his country to three Grand Slams and six Triple Crowns, including four in a row between 1976 and 1979, when he was captain. He also enjoyed the rare distinction of playing in all eight of the Lions Tests in New Zealand (1971) and South Africa (1974) when the tourists won back-to-back rubbers.

It was playing against the English that undoubtedly brought out the best in him. Tries by fullbacks were uncommon before 1969, yet JPR – the three initials were the best-known in the sporting world after LBW – scored five against them. Moreover, he was on the winning side in all eleven of his appearances against the old enemy. How Wales wish they could say that of a player today!

Jonah Lomu

If Jonny Wilkinson was the man who stamped his name on the 2003 Rugby World Cup tournament, the honours at the 1995 and 1999 finals certainly went to the man-mountain from New Zealand, Jonah Lomu.

He was a monster in rugby kit. Relatively unknown in 1995, Lomu became a household name after scoring seven tries – four against England in the semis – to create a new record for the finals. At 6′ 4″ and scaling 19 stone he filled the hearts of opponents with terror – ask Tony Underwood and several others from the 1995 England side who were steamrollered 45–29 by Lomu and the All Blacks.

Originally a back-row forward as a schoolboy, he was converted to a wing before becoming the youngest New Zealand Test player of all time when he made his international debut against France in 1994. He had clocked 10.8 seconds for the hundred metres and the sight of him on the run, ball waving in one hand as he bounced would-be tacklers off his ample body, provided the abiding memory of the 1995 World Cup, when New Zealand coasted to the final only to be defeated in **extra time** by the host nation, South Africa.

Lomu was again the man of the tournament when the World Cup circus rolled into Britain, Ireland and France four years later, but a weak New Zealand side were ambushed by France in a memorable semifinal at Twickenham and Lomu's chance of a winners' medal vanished.

Illness, injury and loss of form ruled him out of the 2003 finals in Australia. England (among others) breathed a massive sigh of relief at this news, but rugby lovers the world over mourned the absence of one of rugby's greatest icons.

Serge Blanco

The man who typified the *joie de vivre* of French rugby throughout France's domination of the Five Nations Championship in the 1980s was Serge Blanco.

He was without doubt a class player whose commitment to adventure and enjoyment was unshakeable. His maxim was that attack was the best form of defence and the sight of Blanco ghosting out of his own half to initiate another move was an image that cheered sports-worshippers of all denominations – not just rugby enthusiasts.

In a career spanning a dozen seasons he became the world's most-capped player, making 93 Test appearances. His remarkable pace took him to 38 tries in internationals during a period when French rugby advanced to the edge of greatness. During his career France won the Grand Slam twice, took or shared the International Championship title six times, and reached the first-ever Rugby World Cup final, in 1987. It was his last-minute lunge for the corner in the semifinal against Australia that brought the try that put the French into that inaugural final.

Right to the end of his rugby career his love of the unexpected was passionate. None will ever forget the champagne moment at Twickenham in 1991 in a Grand Slam showdown when he launched an attack from his own dead-ball line. The play flowed along the right touchline before a cross kick found Philippe Saint-André unmarked in midfield. The wing gathered to score under England's posts. By his role in that famous score, Blanco confirmed his standing as one of the game's legends.

Jeremy Guscott

The player whose inventiveness and silky skills placed him planes above his worldwide rivals in the outside-centre position for the decade from 1989 was Jeremy Guscott. He hit the England side running with four tries on his debut as stand-in for the injured Will Carling against Romania in Bucharest in 1989, and went on to form with Carling an outstandingly successful midfield partnership in three Grand Slam wins.

Although his defensive qualities were sometimes questioned early in his career, Guscott had no superior as an attacker. He could run and kick exquisitely, but it was for his creation of openings for others, most notably Rory Underwood, that he won the hearts of Twickenham crowds. He could rip through packed defences before invariably completing a move by giving a perfectly timed scoring pass. Some tend to forget that his clear-cut breaks also brought him a staggering thirty tries in an England shirt.

He played in two winning series with the Lions. As a youngster he was pitched into the second Test against Australia in Brisbane in 1989 after the tourists had been well beaten in the opening match of the rubber. His penetrative kicking and alertness lent assurance to the three-quarter line and his chip and chase, five minutes from time, brought him the try that sealed a famous win for the Lions. In 1997 in South Africa his towering late dropped goal in the second Test at Durban wrapped up the series in the Lions' favour.

A self-confessed rebel as a teenager, Guscott grew into a relaxed and easy-going character outside rugby. He said he owed much to Bath, his only club during a career that often saw him targeted by Rugby League scouts. Certainly the role models at the club helped mould a personality that had an iron will to succeed both on and off the pitch.

Since retiring he has become a successful rugby analyst for the BBC and his thoughts on the game make interesting reading in the *Sunday Times*.

Cliff Morgan

The automatic choice as Wales fly half in the 1950s was the Rhondda's Cliff Morgan. He played 29 times to set a record (that stood for nearly forty years) as his country's most-capped player in the position.

Early in his career his kicking was a weakness, but he more than compensated for that with his quick-wittedness as a runner. He was a shrewd tactician who showed his ability as an option-taker as early as his second season in the Welsh side. Morgan's tactical control of the Welsh midfield in 1952 was a telling factor in the Grand Slam triumph and his sharp change of pace when sensing openings set up important tries in the tough away wins against both England and Ireland that year.

A huge box-office attraction throughout his career, Morgan steered Wales to three more Championship titles (1954 shared, 1955 shared and 1956 outright when he was captain) and was the spark that ignited the Cardiff and Wales back divisions to memorable victories over the All Blacks in 1953. He also flourished on the firm South African grounds with the 1955 Lions, his electric displays sending spectators into raptures. He captained the Lions in two of the Test matches of a shared rubber with the Springboks.

Off the field he was much in demand. When the Lions landed in South Africa on the 1955 tour he led an impromptu choral session among the players. The South African press announced: 'This is the best team ever to visit these shores,' even before the Lions had played a match.

To the astonishment of his followers, however, he retired young (aged only 27) in 1958. He sensed that some of his sting had evaporated and chose to quit while still in his prime. Morgan never regretted the decision.

When he finished playing, he was snaffled up by the BBC and in a successful career with the corporation went on to head up their outside broadcasts section. He was also one of the original resident captains when the long-running *Question of Sport* quiz was launched in the early 1970s.

Bill Beaumont

The player who more than any other was responsible for England's rugby revival in 1980 was the British bulldog from Fylde and

Lancashire, Bill Beaumont. He came into the side in the mid-1970s and soon commanded a regular place through his technical expertise and special skills as a front-of-the line jumper.

It was the quality of his captaincy, however, that was to drive up England's rugby stock. He stepped in as leader in 1978 and quickly showed his knack for player management. Never one to bawl out his players, Beaumont set about establishing a good team spirit in the belief that mutual respect on the field grew from trust and good relations formed off it.

Players warmed to his example and results steadily improved. With the nucleus of his successful Lancashire county side he led the Northern Division to a famous victory over the 1979 All Blacks before his rebuilding work with England reached its peak in 1980. A national side bursting with the confidence instilled by Beaumont carried off its first Grand Slam for 23 years.

Beaumont was the natural choice as leader of the 1980 Lions to South Africa, becoming the first Englishman for fifty years to enjoy that honour. His side was unlucky to lose the series 3–1. The shorter tour telescoped the four internationals into six weekends with the result that the Lions had little opportunity early in the tour to find their strongest partnerships and combinations.

He remained as England's captain for another two years until he was advised on medical grounds to take early retirement after leading his nation on a then record 21 occasions. It was a disappointing way for one of England's finest rugby servants to depart from the game he deeply loved.

He was another in the line of retired rugby players to occupy a resident captain's chair in the quiz programme *A Question of Sport*.

Barry John

Successful sides need a player who can take a tight game by the scruff of the neck and turn it in their favour. Barry John filled that role in the team that set out to dominate the Five Nations in 1969.

His game was near-perfect. Defenders were left for dead as he jinked, sidestepped or subtly changed pace to drift through heavy traffic. His scores against Scotland and England in the 1969 Triple Crown season were typical John efforts. He was a No. 10 who exhibited ghostlike qualities as he spirited his way to the line, quite unlike the quicksilver outside-halves Cliff Morgan, David Watkins and Phil Bennett who came before and after him.

John was also an exquisite kicker. He had the ability to land a tactical punt on a sixpence and later in his career became the then leading Welsh points scorer of all time (ninety), thanks to his no-nonsense round-the-corner kicking.

An unlikely aspect of his game helped Wales to the 1971 Grand Slam in the match with France in Paris. John would be the first to admit that tackling wasn't his strength, but in taking out big Benoît Dauga as France threatened to score he underlined his bravery. Typically, he complemented his defensive part by making a classic outside-half break for the try that paved the way to victory.

In New Zealand with the 1971 Lions he was the standout player among an outstanding team. His tactical alertness and brilliant kicking – from out of the hand as well as place-kicking – had the All Blacks on the run throughout the series. The Lions became the only British/Irish side to date to win a rubber over there and for his efforts the New Zealand public christened John 'The King'. But the hero-worship, in New Zealand as well as back home in Britain, was not to his liking and less than a year after that tour, like Cliff Morgan before him, he left his followers wanting more when, aged only 27, he chose to retire suddenly.

Six rugby people with names from Shakespeare

Bertram   Count of Rousillon in *All's Well That Ends Well* and Scotland's hooker between 1922 and 1924.

Cranmer   Archbishop of Canterbury in *King Henry VIII* and England centre (1934–38), who later wrote about rugby for the *Sunday Times*.

Hamlet   Prince of Denmark and Ireland's leading cap-winner, in the first decade of the twentieth century.

King John   Eponymous troublesome protagonist of the historical play and nickname coined by New Zealanders for Welsh outside half Barry John, who famously troubled the All Blacks on the 1971 Lions tour.

> **Orlando** Rosalind's lover in *As You Like It* and Italian prop, who appeared in the 2004 and 2005 Six Nations Championship.
>
> **Travers** Retainer of the Earl of Northumberland in *King Henry IV – Part Two* and father-and-son combination who hooked for Wales (1903–11 and 1937–49 respectively).

Rory Underwood

Time and again the player who turned matches in England's favour during the successful early 1990s was the Leicester flyer, Rory Underwood. A surge of pace and the instinctive genius for popping up in the right place at the right time would enable him to take a vital pass and dash over in the corner for a match-breaking try.

Arguably the most important he scored was the one against France that clinched the 1991 Grand Slam. The forwards had made inroads into French territory before Simon Hodgkinson shipped a pass to Underwood wide out on the left. With plenty still to do, the wing accelerated effortlessly on a wide arc around his opponent to score in the corner.

Underwood announced his retirement in 1992, a decision he revoked a couple of months later in order to return to England colours to line up with his brother Tony on England's other wing. It was a happy partnership that lasted three years through to the 1995 Grand Slam, when England played their best rugby of the decade.

He was an ever-present for the Lions in their winning series in Australia in 1989 and scored the try of the match when the 1993 tourists enjoyed their finest hour by beating the All Blacks 20–7 in the second Test in Wellington. When he finally retired in 1996, Rory Underwood had collected numerous England Test records with the unassuming modesty that rugby followers expect of their heroes. Even so, his forty-nine tries and eighty-five caps in a period that included three Grand Slams were England career records that were richly deserved.

Gerald Davies

There was something of his sharpness off the mark, stabbing sidesteps that turned defences inside out or exceptional pace about most of the tries Gerald Davies scored for Wales in a career that spanned Welsh rugby's honour-laden years between 1966 and 1978. When he finally retired, he was the most-capped Welsh three-quarter (forty-six) of all time and shared with Gareth Edwards the then national record for most Test tries (twenty).

He began his career in the centre and his initial tries for Wales came in the match against England in 1967. First, he showed his blistering pace to race clear for a try under the posts. Then the famous Davies shimmy created the space for him to sprint diagonally for the corner to finish the scoring.

Arguably his most memorable deeds, however, came after transferring to the wing on Wales's tour of New Zealand and Australia in 1969. After taking a sabbatical from representative rugby to concentrate on his studies at Cambridge, he accelerated back into the Welsh side for the 1971 Grand Slam year, opening his new account with two more tries against England at Cardiff and scoring the vital late try at Murrayfield against Scotland.

Davies had been a centre with the 1968 Lions in South Africa but was at the peak of his powers on the wing with the Lions in New Zealand in 1971. He scored three tries in the Test series triumphs as well as four in one afternoon against Hawke's Bay.

For seven seasons as a wing he helped Wales hold sway over the Five Nations. When Davies was in possession, the threat was obvious; but even without the ball opponents needed to train several pairs of defenders' eyes on his wing. His like has not been seen for Wales for nearly thirty years.

David Duckham

Strongly built, fast and a graceful runner who could leave defenders standing with his electric sidestep, David Duckham was the most powerful and exciting runner in the British game in the early 1970s. He had no equal for sheer zest and it was his misfortune that he appeared at a time when English rugby was in the doldrums.

Even so, his incisive running was an integral part of several famous England wins. True, sometimes his play lacked vision, but the element of surprise in his attacks often embarrassed opponents. The French, in particular, were left to rue their failure to deal with him in the 1973 match at Twickenham. That day, Duckham thrilled the home crowd (as he had done on foreign fields for the outstanding 1971 Lions and later the Barbarians) with his tricky running and collected two tries to sink French Championship hopes.

At length, England went on to claim their share in a unique quintuple tie in the Championship, each of the Five Nations winning their two home matches but failing away. Later the same year he was a part of England's famous defeat of the All Blacks in Auckland.

He retired as England's most-capped three-quarter in 1976. If his achievements for his country look modest in retrospect, he seemed to epitomise the spirit of running rugby that uplifted British credentials in his time.

What about this Clive Woodward bloke?

Good question. Now he is best known as Sir Clive Woodward, the manager and head coach who steered England to victory in the 2003 Rugby World Cup in Australia. But long before those heady days of success he was a noted player who won twenty-one caps for England.

Woodward made his debut as a centre in the 1980 Grand Slam campaign under Bill Beaumont and was a Lion in South Africa under the same captain later that year, playing in two Tests. He was a Lion again in New Zealand in 1983 before settling for five years in Australia and turning out for the Manly club in Sydney.

He returned to England and reinvented himself as a successful coach. As a player he had been a mercurial centre who thrilled spectators with match-winning talents. He was not afraid to take on opponents, invariably beating them for pace with a searing outside break. England's supporters warmed to his beautifully balanced running.

Those same mercurial qualities marked him out as one of the top-flight coaches in Britain and in 1997 he was appointed in succession to Jack Rowell as coach of the England side that played Australia, New Zealand (twice) and South Africa in the autumn's home internationals. It was a baptism of fire. England lost two and drew two, but his methodical approach and innovations carried the players with him. True, many of his ideas did not come off, but overall his readiness to back players and take chances – in selection and match planning – was the hallmark of his success.

It was Clive Woodward who threw Jonny Wilkinson into the deep end of international rugby, the teenaged Wilkinson becoming the youngest England player for seventy-one years when he made his debut in 1998. England were unsuccessful in the 1999 World Cup, losing to South Africa in an infamous quarterfinal defeat, but Woodward's resolve and the RFU's patience in sticking with him were to pay handsome dividends in 2003.

By the time the next Rugby World Cup came round, Woodward's team had a string of Triple Crown successes and a Grand Slam to their credit, but more importantly they had put together an impressive run of wins – at home and away – against the Tri-Nations. Woodward's side were hot favourites for the 2003 tournament and duly collected the sport's ultimate prize.

Thereafter there was a falling out with his RFU employers and Woodward – now Sir Clive after the World Cup campaign – resigned as England manager in 2004 to concentrate on preparing the 2005 Lions for their visit to New Zealand. There, his golden touch deserted him and the Lions were whitewashed by an out-standing All Blacks side in the Test series.

Woodward briefly took up a management position with Southampton FC, football having been a lifelong passion, but in 2006 he moved on to become director of elite performance with the British Olympic Association. There, he is involved with the panoply of Olympic coverage – thirty-five sports in all – and is responsible for Britain's preparation camp for the 2008 Games to be staged in Beijing.

9.
Twickenham and Other Famous Grounds

Twickenham – the game's Mecca

Twickenham on an international day is *the* place to go to enjoy and appreciate the full meaning of Rugby Union. English supporters at a rugby match are a joy to behold. From their wit and antics in the pubs and restaurants in the Twickenham and Whitton areas to the champagne and sumptuous picnics at the ground's spacious car parks, the English (and their welcome guests) can be seen giving an object lesson in how to enjoy a big sporting occasion with style. Vast quantities of good food and drink will be consumed, yet without the bad manners or grotesque behaviour that sometimes attend other big sporting occasions.

Then, as kickoff in the big match approaches, the pubs and car parks will empty as if called by the Pied Piper, and the multitudes will throng into their seats in the stadium. Segregation among fans is not required here – nor, indeed, at any Rugby Union event. True, the English followers will enjoy the game more if England win; but if not, what the hell? They will return to their pubs and the car parks to continue revelling good-naturedly into the night.

Six famous inhabitants of Twickenham

Henry Fielding Writer, playwright and journalist. The son of this 'great, tattered bard' was baptised in Twickenham in 1748.

Sir Godfrey Kneller The portrait painter was a church-warden at Twickenham Church and is buried there. His home is now known as Kneller Hall, the home of the Royal Military School of Music – just a touch kick beyond the rugby stadium's West Stand.

Brian May The *Queen* guitarist was born in Twickenham in 1947 and rehearsed as a teenager at Chase Bridge Primary School, a pitch-length from the rugby ground's West Car Park.

Alexander Pope The oft-quoted poet and translator of Homer settled in Twickenham in 1719, building a villa near the river.

J M W Turner The landscape painter lived in Sandycombe Road, Twickenham and took his inspiration for many of his works from the river.

Horace Walpole The son of Britain's first Prime Minister settled there in his thirties, acquiring a 5-acre smallholding in Strawberry Hill that he developed into a 46-acre estate.

The ground did not become the headquarters – or **HQ** – of English rugby until the early 1900s. Until then, England staged their home games at a variety of club grounds up and down the country. It was an RFU committeeman named Billy Williams who earmarked a market-garden site in what was then described as 'the picturesque Middlesex village' as a possible home for English rugby.

The Union purchased it in 1907 and the ground, with accommodation for about 20,000 spectators, was ready to stage its first international in 1910. It was known as 'Billy Williams' cabbage patch' in its early days, but in deference to the RFU's high standing in the politics of world rugby it became better known as HQ, an expression that later became associated with the late Peter West, a broadcaster and writer who seemed to epitomise the Twickenham rugby scene for forty years after World War II.

The ground has undergone many refurbishments in the hundred years since it was purchased, and the most ambitious development is the current facelift at the south end of the ground backing the Whitton Road. Down the years the RFU have purchased a number of the old Victorian and Edwardian villas lining the road, using them as pieds-à-terre for a number of their staff before multi-purpose office accommodation was developed in the latter years of the twentieth century.

In 2006 a row of the houses was demolished to make way for the multi-tiered south stand that now completely encloses the Twickenham pitch; behind the stand a luxury hotel with a hundred-plus rooms has been planned. The ultimate in rugby weekends will become a three-day stay-over at the hotel with tickets for a Grand Slam decider at the ground.

The marketing arm of the RFU's operation has shrewdly made its merchandise available at the ground outside match weekends, and tours of the ground are available to members of the public on weekdays. The tour includes a ticket for the RFU's museum, which has arguably the most complete collection of rugby memorabilia anywhere in the world. It is well worth a visit to see early match programmes and film of famous matches dating back to the era immediately before World War I.

Particularly amusing is the silent movie of the 1911 England–France match staged at the ground. Watch the England team amble onto the pitch exchanging banter with the moustachioed Welsh referee attired in overcoat and scarf. Almost certainly one of the players is smoking a cigarette as he comes onto the field – all very relaxed and different from the intensity of today's international matches.

Six other activities at Twickenham Stadium

1906 The ground and its environs was an orchard and market garden in what was described as a 'picturesque Middlesex village'. One year later it was nicknamed 'Billy Williams' Cabbage Patch' after the RFU committeeman who earmarked the site as the future home of English rugby.

1916 Used as farmland during World War I, it was a grazing area for sheep, cattle and horses.

1944 The West Stand was damaged by a V-bomb. During the war the ground was requisitioned and occupied by the Civil Defence. It was returned to agricultural use as part of the 'Dig for Victory' campaign and all the iron railings and crush barriers were removed for scrap metal.

1974 Streaking made its debut when Michael O'Brien stripped off at the England–Wales match and PC Perry instigated a police cover-up with his helmet. Much more memorable, though, were the titters at Twickers caused by Erika Roe nearly eight years later at half-time in the England–Australia game.

2000 Rugby League's World Cup opened with an England–Australia tie at the ground.

2006 The Rolling Stones performed on the pitch as part of their *Bigger Bang* tour.

Cardiff

Ask a Welsh rugby fan the name of the rugby ground in Cardiff and the answer will almost certainly give away their age. Anyone over 45 will give the *correct* answer: Cardiff Arms Park; those between 30 and 45 will probably answer the National Ground, while the younger generation will refer to it as the Millennium Stadium.

Back in the mid-1800s the area was a park behind the old Cardiff Arms Hotel, a coaching inn in the (then) town centre and adjacent to the River Taff – indeed, the park bordered the river and often flooded. The great engineer, Isambard Kingdom Brunel, was engaged in 1848 to divert the course of the river in order to accommodate the railway and it was land reclaimed from the Taff that became known as the Cardiff Arms Park.

Cardiff Cricket Club were the first group to occupy the area for organised sport, and when rugby became popular in Wales later in the century many of the cricketers formed the Cardiff Rugby Club.

In 1884, the ground staged its first international when Wales defeated Ireland, and in 1893 Wales launched their first Triple Crown campaign there with a one-point victory over England. Indeed, England did not win in Cardiff until 1913, and between 1963 and 1991 made thirteen successive visits to the Welsh capital without success.

Even so, the most famous Welsh win came in 1905 when the first All Blacks, at the end of an unbeaten tour through England, Scotland and Ireland, lost 3–0 there. That was the day when the Welsh national anthem 'Hen Wlad Fy Nhadau' was sung as an impromptu response to the New Zealand **haka**. The atmosphere, it was reported, was electric as the singing moved the Welsh team to a magnificent achievement. The anthem became forever associated with Welsh rugby and features at the top of the bill on the Cardiff singing programme on international match days.

It was also in the year 1905 that city status was conferred on Cardiff, and of all the great rugby cities worldwide, not one can point to a national rugby ground that lies so close to its centre. Cardiff Central, the main-line station that delivers supporters to the capital on big match days, is just a five-minute walk from the ground. And in the days of hot metal, the rugby critic of Wales's national newspaper, Bryn Thomas, had only to cross the road to take up his place in the press box at home internationals. For thirty-six years he covered Welsh rugby for the Cardiff *Western Mail* at minimum expense – at least as far as home games were concerned.

In the late 1960s a marathon refurbishment of the ground was undertaken. With both Cardiff and Wales sharing the Arms Park, the pitch became a mud bath by midwinter and was a real drawback to the type of running rugby the Welsh enjoyed playing and their supporters enjoyed watching.

It took over a decade to build the new stadium and during a period of outstanding Welsh success on the field, not a single match was transferred from Cardiff, though admittedly the place sometimes resembled a building site when games took place.

Cardiff RFC moved next door to occupy the area previously used by Glamorgan County Cricket Club and the playing surface was transformed into one of the best in Britain. The promoters changed its title to the National Stadium, but the die-hards continued to think of it as the Cardiff Arms Park. Then, less than fifteen years after the great master plan had been delivered, three-quarters of the ground was demolished again to make way for a modern state-of-the-art stadium fit for the twenty-first century.

The focus for this redevelopment was the staging of the 1999 Rugby World Cup in Wales. As part of the plan, the playing area was turned through a right angle and the three sides that were knocked down rose out of the rubble to form the magnificent Millennium Stadium. The work was completed on schedule – retractable roof and all – so that even the worst of Wales's notoriously wet days will no longer affect the rugby.

But the old-timers still think of it as the Cardiff Arms Park.

Murrayfield

The Scottish Rugby Union (SRU) used to be renowned for their conservatism in all matters to do with Rugby Union. In the early years of the twentieth century, for instance, they harboured suspicions of professionalism relating to expense payments surrounding the early major touring sides, and because of this did not sanction any matches against the first Wallabies (1908–9) and refused to participate in the proposed British tour of Australia and New Zealand in 1908.

Later, they were the last Union to permit their players to wear numbers in international matches. Indeed, there is a story that King George V, while shaking hands with a Scottish team visiting Twickenham as late as 1928, enquired of the SRU's special representative, one James Aikman Smith, why the Scots were numberless.

His Majesty received short shrift from the esteemed Scottish official. 'This is a rugby match, not a cattle sale,' he was told.

It might seem strange, therefore, to relate that the Scots were actually the first Union to realise the importance of purchasing and establishing their own home ground for international matches, and to that extent bought and developed the Inverleith ground in

Edinburgh as early as 1896–7, financing their development by the issue of **debentures**.

From 1899 – some ten years before Twickenham opened as the home of English international rugby – until the early 1920s Scotland played most of their matches on their Union's own ground. Then in 1925, the Union, recognising the need to accommodate greater crowds as interest in Rugby Union expanded, purchased the Murrayfield site to the west of the city.

The ground was initially surrounded by three giant terraces with a grandstand along the touchline that housed the SRU's offices. The first match staged there coincided with Scotland's first-ever Grand Slam triumph, a 14–11 victory over England. Extensions to the main stand were added in 1936, doubling seating capacity to 15,000.

But the vast majority were accommodated on the giant terraces, and with the ground's considerable space, entry was relatively relaxed, with all internationals until the late 1970s being pay-at-the-gate affairs.

For the Welsh match in 1975, however, such a huge contingent of Welshmen travelled north for the Murrayfield weekend that the ground was overwhelmed. Matters were not helped by the collapse of a perimeter fence behind the touchline terrace, and the official estimate of 104,000 (who passed through the turnstiles) was expanded unofficially to 111,000 for gate-crashers – easily the record attendance for any International Championship match. After that, the SRU made all international matches all-ticket affairs on health and safety grounds.

An interesting innovation had been made in 1959 with the laying of an underground electric blanket. The undersoil heating ensured that rugby's most northern capital city could always guarantee that its international match could go ahead, and never was the blanket of more use than four years later when, in 1963, both the Scotland–Wales and Scotland–Ireland matches went ahead in a season of sustained adverse weather conditions.

Nowadays the ground is an all-seater stadium and completely enclosed. It is also one of the most comfortable complexes in the world for spectators, with good uninterrupted views from almost every seat in the ground. Although the ground is not as central as Cardiff Arms Park is to the Welsh capital, the SRU's home is a manageable walk from Edinburgh Waverley main-line station and the famous Princes Street in Edinburgh's city centre.

Lansdowne Road

The Dublin home of Irish rugby is the oldest stadium in the world to still stage Rugby Union internationals. Originally the ground was the long-lease property of one Henry Dunlop, a keen athlete who earmarked the site for athletics championships. In 1876, an athletics international between England and Ireland was staged there – the first-ever athletics meeting between nations – and in 1878 the ground hosted its first rugby international.

The Lansdowne RFC were tenants from the time Dunlop took out his long lease on the ground and that club did much to enhance amenities and improve the playing surface, including an early decision to turn the pitch through a right angle.

In 1927, the first-ever concrete stand with terrace accommodation underneath was built in Ireland when the old grandstand on the eastern side of the ground was demolished. The crowd sheltering in its uncovered 'shell' during that season's Ireland–Scotland fixture endured the most awful conditions as rain lashed in from the Irish Sea. One of the Irish players, it was reported, had to be treated for hypothermia, so severe were the conditions.

But Lansdowne Road's great charm has always been its welcome and, from the start, visiting international teams enjoyed the pre-match tension and after-match celebrations. It was for that reason that the Irish Union remained loyal to Lansdowne and never seriously considered staging Dublin internationals elsewhere.

There is a warm and uniquely homely atmosphere to international days at Lansdowne Road. Part of the reason for this is the fact that a large number of Ireland's top clubs have their headquarters within walking distance of the ground. Indeed two clubs, Lansdowne and Wanderers, share the ground, while a short walk away another two of Dublin's best-known teams, Bective Rangers and Old Wesley, have their clubhouses at either end of the famous Donnybrook ground. Clubs are open to members and friends only, of course, but typically all the Dublin clubs have huge numbers of friends visiting on international weekends. Irish hospitality is always irresistible and none would argue with the maxim that the best supporters when they win at home are the Irish, and the best supporters when they lose at home . . . are the Irish.

The ground lease was later taken on by the Irish Rugby Union, though just over a century passed before they were actually able to buy the freehold in the mid-1970s. The ground underwent numerous refurbishments during that time, including the building of substantial concrete stands along both touchlines, but by the end of the millennium it was clear that 'the old grey stadium' was in need of a considerable face-lift to bring it into the twenty-first century.

From 2007, while Lansdowne Road is closed for two years, the Irish Rugby Union has had to up sticks from the south of the city and move their home internationals north to the Gaelic Athletic Association's (GAA) headquarters at Croke Park. The new stage for international rugby in Dublin has been the GAA's home since 1884, though it did not purchase the site until 1913, paying £3,500 for it. For years 'British' sports were banned from the site, but it underwent extensive refurbishment between 1994 and 2004 and Ireland will play all their home internationals there (in front of capacity crowds of 82,300) until Lansdowne Road is completed in 2009.

But rest assured, despite the magnificent rugby spectacles that 'Croker' witnessed when Ireland played France and England there in 2007, normal service will eventually be resumed at Lansdowne Road. There, 50,000 – the same capacity as before the ground was closed for redevelopment – will sit in comfort to enjoy uninterrupted views of the ground and watch Ireland extend the warm hand of welcome to its rugby adversaries.

Stade de France

French sports grounds are municipally owned and their national stadia are no exception to this rule. France's regular home venue – for Rugby Union and soccer internationals – until 1972 was Stade Colombes in the northwestern suburbs of the city. The ground was developed for the 1924 'Chariots of Fire' Olympic Games but gave way in 1973 to the concrete bowl of the Parc des Princes near the southwestern edge of the city's périphérique intérieur.

The Stade de France was built in the northern Paris suburb of St Denis for the 1998 soccer World Cup (won by France) and it will be the venue for Rugby's World Cup final later this year. It staged its first rugby international (France v England) in February 1998, Christophe Dominici scoring a try on his debut and Thomas

Castaignède dropping a goal in a win that set France on the way to the Grand Slam.

The capacity is 80,000 – nearly double that of Parc des Princes, which will also be extensively used during the forthcoming Rugby World Cup. There is a direct rail link to St Denis and Stade de France is a ten-minute walk from Porte de Paris metro station.

All of France's national rugby grounds have been noisy cauldrons. Players find it difficult hearing **calls** when playing in Paris. A special feature of French home internationals (and, sometimes, their away games, too) is the various brass-band-playing collections of spectators who travel to the matches. Listen out for the Dax Band strike up during an exciting piece of French play. If it's quiet in Paris, France are losing.

Stadio Olimpico, Rome

The Roman weekend is a must for all Six Nations aficionados – the sights, the climate, the food and the wine. Yet the Italians' home ground is the smallest on the Championship's circuit, with a capacity of 25,000. Situated in the city's northern quarter, the stadium was built in 1959 as part of the developments for the Rome Olympics in 1960. It staged its first-ever Six Nations match when Italy joined the championship in February 2000. Diego Dominguez inspired the Azzurri to beat Scotland 34–20 that day.

Players find the pitch in Rome narrower than most international grounds. This puts a restriction on open tactics but gives a distinct advantage to the strong forward-oriented game favoured by Italy.

Ellis Park, Johannesburg

The Ellis in the home of South African rugby has no connection whatsoever with William Webb Ellis. The Mr Ellis whose name adorns this stadium was a humble local councillor who fought tooth and nail for the original open site to retain its recreational aspect when developers wanted to buy it for housing.

It was the Transvaal Rugby Union who acquired the plot in the late 1920s and converted it into international rugby's highest ground above sea level. In 1928 South Africa entertained New Zealand, their great rivals, in the first of the ground's famous Test matches and it has become the Mecca for all rugby fans visiting the Republic.

It was there in 1938 that Vivian Jenkins, the Lions fullback, kicked one of the longest penalty goals in history. His altitude-assisted effort from inside his own half flew fully sixty-five metres, but could not win the Test for the Lions.

When the Welshman returned there in 1955, as the first Fleet Street journalist to cover a full Lions' rugby tour, he witnessed one of the most breathtaking Tests in the history of the game. In the region of 95,000 spectators were present, a then world record for a rugby match of any kind, to see the Lions, in the opening match of their four-Test rubber, beat the Springboks 23–22 in a real nailbiter of a match. South Africa struck back with a try scored in the last minute, but their veteran fullback Jack van der Schyff failed to add the conversion points that would have brought victory.

South Africans, however, have no doubt about the greatest rugby game played there. It was in June 1995 when the Rainbow Nation, led by François Pienaar on the field and Nelson Mandela off it (but each wearing the Springbok No. 6 jersey), lifted the Rugby World Cup at their first attempt.

During the apartheid years they had been banned from competing in the tournament so did not appear in the first two World Cups in 1987 and 1991. But their entry in 1995 culminated in an extra-time victory, thanks to a memorable dropped goal by outside half Joel Stransky.

Eden Park, Auckland

The home of New Zealand rugby was the scene of the first Rugby World Cup final in 1987 and of innumerable All Black rugby triumphs down the years since it staged its first international in 1921, against South Africa.

The All Blacks were beaten by the Springboks that day, but they coasted to victory against France in that inaugural World Cup final and will probably do so again when the event is scheduled to return there for its seventh tournament in 2011.

It is a feature of many major rugby grounds in New Zealand (as it used to be in Australia) that they double as Test cricket venues. Imagine Lord's staging an England v New Zealand rugby match in the autumn and a cricket Test match the next summer. Far-fetched? Maybe, yet that is precisely what happens without fazing the groundsmen at Eden Park.

Six notable rugby attendances

109,874 The current world record for an international match: Australia–New Zealand at Stadium Australia in 2000.

107,042 Australia–New Zealand 1999. The first rugby international staged in Stadium Australia, the complex built for the 2000 Olympic Games in Sydney.

104,000 The record attendance for an International Championship match: Scotland–Wales 1975 at Murrayfield on St David's Day. (The 'unofficial' crowd figure was 111,000.)

95,000 South Africa–British & Irish Lions 1955 at Ellis Park, Johannesburg. The first 90,000-plus attendance for a Rugby Union match.

95,000 Romania–France 1957 at the August 23rd Stadium, Bucharest. The crowd had assembled for a major soccer match and stayed on to cheer the Romanian rugby side to a near victory over the French, who eventually won 18–15 through a late penalty goal.

30 And this is the world record for the fewest spectators at an international match: United States–South Africa in 1981 at Owl Creek Polo Field, Glenville, New York. The match venue was kept a secret to avoid unwanted apartheid demonstrators. The teams, allegedly, had to clear the polo field of horse manure before the rugby match could be staged.

10.
What Media Coverage Does Rugby Get?

Which critics and newspapers should I read . . . or avoid?

The game enjoys good coverage in the former broadsheets and the correspondents who lead their newspapers' rugby columns write knowledgeably and critically, but with an overriding love for their sport.

The newspaper of record in the United Kingdom is the title that has traditionally gone to *The Times*, and in David Hands – only their fourth chief rugby correspondent in over ninety years – that distinction is proudly upheld. Hands is the most accurate recorder of the game and his Monday morning reflections on the weekend's matches should be compulsory reading.

It is a shame that the sports desk at this newspaper cannot find more space for Rugby Union, especially in the summer when coverage is haphazard and details of the important Tri-Nations matches are quite often omitted.

The *Daily Telegraph*, by contrast, pulls out all the stops to bring its readers comprehensive coverage of the rugby scene all year round. Its writers, led by Mick Cleary and ably supported by the enthusiastic Brendan Gallagher and Rob Wildman, comprise the best rugby-writing team among the dailies. The *Independent* and the *Guardian* run them close, with Peter Jackson and Steve Bale maintaining the *Daily Mail* and the *Express*'s excellent reputations as a good rugby read.

Sunday journalism is a different art. Tight Saturday evening deadlines are not helped by the increasing trend (dictated by television scheduling) for evening kickoffs. But for anyone wanting to tap in to rugby's current state Stephen Jones of the *Sunday Times* is the man to read. His stories and acuteness in reading a match (often within minutes of its completion, so tight are the deadlines) put his newspaper at the top of the Rugby Union reader's list.

Former players are often in demand by newspapers looking to boost their circulation. Paul Ackford, the outstanding England lock of the early Will Carling era, is head and shoulders (literally and literately) above the rest in this category and his team at the *Sunday Telegraph*, which includes the whimsical Rupert Bates, should also be required reading. Eddie Butler, whose sharp-witted observations adorn the *Observer*, is another ex-international forward who successfully swapped the **sweatband** for the pen.

What are the important books about the game?

Rugby Union has never produced anything that approaches the literature that cricket enjoys. There is no rugby equivalent of the late Sir Neville Cardus, the former *Guardian* cricket correspondent whose elegant prose enchanted generations of cricket followers.

The best rugby writer of the past thirty years was the late John Reason. He made it his business to get to know the leading players as well as selectors and administrators, and he became a trenchant critic whose columns were forthright and honest. A former *Telegraph* rugby correspondent, he penned several Lions tour books and among his output were two of the game's classics.

The Lions Speak was a distillation of a seminar held by John Dawes and members of the successful 1971 Lions squad that toured New Zealand. Reason was the scribe who turned their words of wisdom into a coaching bible. He later wrote a very readable history of the game, *The World of Rugby*, which was commissioned to complement an excellent BBC television series. His collaborator on this project was Carwyn James, who had coached that famous 1971 Lions side.

Stephen Jones, who regarded Reason's work as 'massively influential', produced two works that tell the inside story of the huge changes rugby has seen in the past fifteen years. His *Endless Winter*, published in 1993, searched for the soul of the game as it headed inexorably towards professionalism, and won the coveted William Hill Sports Book of the Year award. The sequel, *Midnight Rugby*, published nine years later, put the effects of professionalism into sharp perspective.

For a southern hemisphere perspective on recent developments Donald McRae's *Winter Colours* is a racy and rewarding read. Published between Jones's two major efforts, this is a South African's reflection on his country's Rugby World Cup success in 1995 as well as a compendium of views on the game drawn from the game's leading past and present personalities. Great stuff!

Broadcasting

Ex-forwards, it has already been suggested, make the best critics of the game. It could also be argued that they make the best broadcasters too.

From 1927, when the England and Wales game at Twickenham became the first live outside radio broadcast of any sporting event in the United Kingdom, until 1991 the BBC had a monopoly on transmissions of major rugby matches. And for much of that time the name synonymous with rugby broadcasting was Bill McLaren, the former Hawick flanker who had a final trial for Scotland in the late 1940s.

Bill was at Twickenham in 1938 – as a teenager, not commentator – when Scotland beat England in the first-ever televised match shown by the Beeb, and from the early 1950s until his retirement in 2002 he was rarely off broadcasting duty.

Since then Eddie Butler and the former England hooker Brian Moore have provided an amusing commentating double act that is informative and *au fait* with the dark arts of forward play. Former internationals Jonathan Davies, Keith Wood and Jeremy Guscott provide the expert analysis in the studio.

In 1991, ITV won the rights to show the second Rugby World Cup, staged in Britain, Ireland and France. Ex-Wales and Lions flanker John Taylor was the voice of the new order and he has now led the ITV commentary team through four successive World Cup finals. His sidekick at these tournaments has been Steve Smith, England's 1980 Grand Slam scrum half.

Sky Television emerged from Rupert Murdoch's media empire in the 1990s to provide a third major element in the jigsaw of rugby broadcasting. Miles Harrison, their main man, is complemented by the sharp-witted Stuart Barnes, a former England outside half, while Dewi Morris and Michael Lynagh are among the distinguished former players who provide studio analysis.

Sky is the only channel that devotes time to a regular rugby magazine show. *The Rugby Club* is a review and preview programme also featuring a regular tactics slot hosted by Barnes and Morris. The show runs for an hour and a half each week.

For those who prefer their rugby doses in shorter packages then the IRB's weekly *Total Rugby* show, also shown by Sky, is a must. Apart from covering the main rugby events of the week, this fast-moving show includes interesting features from all over rugby's oval world.

And don't forget good old steam radio. Here the former Scotland outside half Ian Robertson and another English ex-international, Alastair Hignell, are supported by Matt Dawson. Eighty years after that first broadcast, the BBC continues to paint word pictures for those who cannot get in front of a television or find a ticket for the match.

Other media

Among the dozen or so rugby periodicals that stand out is the popular monthly *Rugby World*. It will celebrate its fiftieth anniversary at the start of the 2010–11 season, making it the longest-running show currently on the rugby road.

It has reinvented itself to the benefit of the game several times in its first half-century and shows every sign of lasting long into the future, something that cannot be said for many of the publications launched in the past.

These days it wisely concentrates on features, the newspapers having already covered the essential detail of matches long before the magazine hits the bookstalls. The editor is Paul Morgan and he, more than any other member of the media, has done a wonderful job in advancing the burgeoning women's game.

Down the years *Rugby World* has also been responsible for promoting the best in rugby photography. It provided the ideal platform to showcase the talents of a young Colin Elsey in the late 1960s and early 1970s. Elsey, a former Wasps lock, brought sports photography (and especially Rugby Union, which was his passion) into the twentieth century, using the latest technology to produce wonderful action shots. His shot of Lions prop Fran Cotton caked in mud during a match on the 1971 tour of New Zealand was a photographic masterpiece that became a rugby icon.

Elsey, who set up the Colorsport business in London, died on the eve of the 2003 Rugby World Cup, but his pioneering action photography inspired a generation of rugby snappers. Foremost among these are Dave Rogers, Stu Forster and Morgan Treacey, the inaugural winner of the IRB's Rugby Photograph of the Year competition.

Among the new media Scrum.com and planet-rugby.com deserve credit for designing lively and extensive news websites backed up by excellent statistical content. These sites, like the leading magazines, recruit rugby's top correspondents to pen lively columns. There are also informative sites run by the IRB as well as all the major Unions.

Do I need to know any famous statistics?

The late Richard Burton once described rugby as the game of massive lies and stupendous exaggerations. He was referring to the great army of rugby's phoneys – people who claim to have played in a final trial for Ireland or turned out once for Bath in the centre with Jeremy Guscott.

Because rugby lacks an equivalent to cricket's *Wisden* these claims are often impossible to confirm (or refute). Even so, there are some books of record that give the details of international players and results, and for anyone with such an interest the annual *IRB World Rugby Yearbook* is the bible.

Most of the game's records today are held by one J P Wilkinson of England, but one or two other statistics are presented overleaf for general appreciation.

Six of the best rugby statistics

Eric Tindill The New Zealander is the only man who has played Test rugby and Test cricket for his country *and* refereed Test rugby and umpired Test cricket.

1964 The last time a Test match ended scoreless. Scotland and New Zealand shared the draw at Murrayfield (there had also been scoreless Test draws in 1961, 1962 and 1963).

1,090 The most points scored in Test rugby. Neil Jenkins of Wales took ninety-one Tests (including four for the Lions) between 1991 and 2002 to reach that total.

164 The highest score in an official rugby international match. Hong Kong beat Singapore 164–13 in a Rugby World Cup qualifying match in Kuala Lumpur in 1994.

Dr James Marsh The only man who was capped for two different countries in the International Championship. He turned out for England in 1892 and for Scotland in 1889.

Daisuke Ohata In 2006 the Japanese winger overtook Australia's David Campese (sixty-four tries) to become the record-holder for most tries scored in Tests.

For all the major internationals and top club, provincial and regional competitions the media is supplied with an array of statistical information, even down to 'commentator's notes' for televised matches. So any major milestone reached during a game that is broadcast live will be noted. For those attending big matches, programmes invariably flag up the major statistics relating to the fixture.

The first six players to win 100 senior rugby caps for their country

Philippe Sella The Frenchman became Rugby Union's first centurion when he played in a winning side against New Zealand in 1994.

David Campese Australia's maverick wing/fullback was the first southern hemisphere player to join the 100 club, appearing against Italy, the land of his forefathers in Padua in 1996.

Jason Leonard The first representative from the Home Unions and the first forward to play 100 times for his country. England's favourite prop marked the occasion by leading his side out at Twickenham against France in 2003.

George Gregan Australia were the first country to claim two 100-cappers. Their scrum half and captain achieved the distinction in Perth, Western Australia playing against South Africa in the 2004 Tri-Nations.

Fabien Pelous The big French lock won his 100th cap in Dublin in 2005. As captain of France he won the toss, played into a strong wind and led his side to victory. The day before he had celebrated his ton by drinking champagne at a training run-out.

Donna Kennedy The Scottish women's Number Eight reached the milestone in March 2007 – the first woman to achieve the distinction.

11.
So, Am I Ready to Go and Watch a Match Now?

Reading about the theory and lore of the game is all very well, but it's not the same as going to a match. The best place for newcomers to start is at a junior rugby match – the local club's minis or a school match. There are slight variations to the more technical laws that are in force at levels from under-18 down, but the form of the game – passing, kicking, set pieces – and, of course, the pitch markings and scoring actions are common throughout the rugby continuum.

Then join a local rugby club and study the pattern of the senior game by watching the first XV in action. This will help to develop your knowledge of tactics as well as give you an understanding of refereeing.

Getting ready for the game

Rugby is a winter game so warm clothes are usually a necessity. Cushions (often available at the major grounds) and blankets provide extra comforts.

If attending an international match or major club/provincial/ regional fixture, it is a wise idea to take a pair of light binoculars or opera glasses. The major modern rugby stadiums such as Twickenham provide excellent uninterrupted views of the pitch, but it can be akin to watching a Subbuteo match for spectators who are seated at the back of the highest tier of the stands.

A recent innovation at international matches is the 'Ref-link' – a simple headphones device that wires spectators directly to the referee. That way, spectators can hear the referee's decisions and his explanations to players. The links are usually sold within the stadium concourse.

When going to an international match, ensure that your entry ticket is valid and has been purchased through a reputable source – usually an affiliated rugby club. Unions, quite rightly, are stamping down on those who try to resell tickets at hugely inflated prices. These days most of the Unions record precisely where each ticket has been allocated, so any tickets sold on can be tracked. The Unions reserve the right to punish the original sources by denying them priority access to tickets for future big matches. Several players and many leading clubs have had their fingers rapped for passing on tickets that have found their way into the wrong hands.

Try to arrive early. Teams usually arrive at a match venue a couple of hours before the kickoff and usually a buzz goes around the concourse when the teams file off the team bus and walk into the ground. Something of a ritual has been established at Twickenham before big matches, where large crowds gather behind the West Stand to see the players walk from the car park to the RFU's main committee entrance leading to the stands and changing areas. If you think some international players look big on the television, you'll discover they're enormous when seen in the flesh.

Buy a programme or match-day magazine before the game. The teams will be listed inside, there will be features on the players taking part and general articles that can be read to while away the time before kickoff or at half-time. Do not throw the programme away. Mementos of famous matches hold their value and often realise staggering prices at auctions (or even on eBay) among seasoned collectors of rugby memorabilia.

During the game

Home team supporters and visitors sit together at rugby matches. They will exchange banter, pass light-hearted judgement on the players (and referee) and enjoy the thrill of an exciting game. Get involved.

Rugby crowds, which often include many former players, appreciate the finer parts of the game. They often express their approval of a particularly fine piece of play with applause, so join in. Crowds are sporting and appreciate talent, irrespective of which team supplies it.

It is not customary to boo teams, though some ignorant elements do exist at rugby matches and sometimes attempt to disturb the concentration of kickers making attempts to kick goals. Such behaviour is discouraged as discourteous.

Are all spectators potential streakers?

It is true that two of the best-remembered streaks at sporting events were at Twickenham during big international matches broadcast live on television. But fortunately images like those of Michael O'Brien being frogmarched along the touchline and out of the ground during the 1974 England–Wales game, with only a PC's helmet covering his manhood, have not been common at rugby grounds.

Erika Roe's streak eight years later when big Bill Beaumont was leading England against Australia was described by one of the game's august correspondents as 'like a galleon in full sail, but minus her spinnakers'.

Ms Roe had the decency to wait until the game had temporarily ceased for half-time before baring herself in front of the South Stand. Those were the days when players remained on the field for a captain's pep talk at the break.

Beaumont was in full flow, trying to rally his men, when he realised everyone's focus was on a distant apparition. 'What's the problem?' asked the bemused Bill.

'There's a girl over there with your bum on her chest, Bill,' came the reply.

Generally, however, the rule is: Keep your kit on if you want to see the whole of the match.

12.
What Is Rugby Union's Appeal?

The basics and tactics, the game and the players, and the grounds and conventions covered so far in this book give an idea of the theory of Rugby Union. But the real appeal of the game lies in its atmosphere and wit.

Rugby attracts a huge cross section of followers. High Court judges and cabinet ministers rub shoulders with manual workers and postmen; city slickers with public-sector workers. All are attracted by the unique atmosphere that surrounds a game of rugby – before, during and afterwards – and particularly the opportunity to make countless friendships.

The anticipation is as enjoyable as the event itself, especially if one's team wins against the odds. And the game's history, happily, is littered with examples of the surprise element – a team overcoming a hot favourite, for example.

During the 1991 Rugby World Cup tournament, the first to stage matches in the United Kingdom, the unknown Western Samoans made their bow with a pool match against Wales at Cardiff. The Welsh side included Ieuan Evans, Scott Gibbs, Phil Davies and Robert Jones, four of the outstanding rugby players of their generation. Imagine, then, the shock when Wales were trailing for most of the second half and finished the match 16–13 losers to the Pacific Islanders.

The Welsh crowd's reaction was to treat adversity with wit. The choral legions in the old East Terrace, used in earlier decades to greeting their Triple Crown and Grand Slam heroes with hymns and arias, took to whistling the *Monty Python* team's 'Always Look on the Bright Side of Life'.

There were no angry protests from the fans as they left Cardiff to drown their sorrows that Sunday afternoon. Disappointment, yes; but they took their beating with grace and good humour.

'Thank goodness we didn't have to play the whole of Samoa,' said one wag.

The same bonhomie extends to the game at club level. Leicester Tigers are one of the best-supported rugby sides in the land, their supporters having welcomed friend and foe to Welford Road for more than a hundred years.

At the other end of rugby's time spectrum, Watford was a rugby desert fifteen years ago. In 2007, however, the Fez Boys of Saracens celebrated ten years of supporting their side at Watford's Vicarage Road. The group set themselves up with their exclusive headwear to welcome anyone new to watching Sarries, and to encourage Watford's youngsters to get behind the club.

It was an amusing addition to the hugely successful marketing campaign that the late Peter Deakin brought to Saracens towards the end of the 1990s, and the Fez Boys became synonymous with the Watford-based club.

The pre-match and post-match atmosphere is one to soak up – the anticipation or the resignation can quickly be suppressed by the banter that surrounds host and visitor. It is that atmosphere of wit and friendship that makes Rugby Union unique.

It was arguably best summed up by the late Peter Robbins, a former England flanker, one-time *Financial Times* rugby correspondent and bon viveur, as follows:

'What is rugby? It is a strong drink to be sipped slowly and in the company of true friends.'

Everyone in Rugby Union will drink to that.

Glossary

This glossary is provided for quick reference when listening to a radio or television broadcast of a match and for understanding any discussion regarding the game. Readers are not expected to read the section from A to Z.

Brief descriptions are given for words and phrases that are part of rugby's lexicon. The cross references (in **bold**) provide a fuller understanding of some points and keep the original descriptions brief.

This section also doubles as a thesaurus, for quite often more than one word or phrase is used by the rugby fraternity to describe an aspect of the game.

Getting on for 500 entries appear in the list that follows, underlining the complexity of the game. Experts will no doubt delight in pointing out an oversight – a regular piece of jargon that has been overlooked – but hopefully most of the common (and some of the more uncommon) vocabulary of rugby-speak is captured here.

The list includes official language (from the current Law Book, for instance) and colloquialisms (marked *coll*), particularly those commonly used by commentators. The letters *n* (noun) and *vb* (verb) are given where context demands, and where entries have multiple meanings they have been marked with the numbers *1, 2* or *3*.

Accidental offside: Unintentionally touching the ball or the ball-carrier when in an **offside** position.

Added time: Time added at the end of each **half** to ensure that playing time – time that excludes pauses for injuries or directions from the referee – lasts exactly forty minutes.

Advantage law: An important rule that permits referees to use their discretion when an **infringement** has taken place. If a territorial or tactical advantage accrues to the non-offending team, the referee may allow play to continue.

Advantage line: An imaginary line running the width of the pitch through the middle of a scrum, line-out, ruck or maul.

Advantage over: Call made in play by the referee when the **advantage law** has lapsed.

Affiliated: Name given to rugby clubs that are officially recognised by their **Unions**.

Against the tight-head: Winning the ball when the opposition has had the **feed** at a **scrum**.

A international: An international match involving a nation's second-best players.

Air (tackled in the): Illegal (and dangerous) **tackle** on a player whose feet are not on the ground.

Alickadoo: Term unique to Rugby Union for a club or Union committee member.

All Blacks: The men's fifteen-a-side New Zealand international rugby team.

Amateur: One who is not paid for playing Rugby Union (theoretically this referred to every Rugby Union player until 1995 when the game went **open**).

Ankle tap: A legal trip made with the hand.

Attacking side: The opponents of the **defending team**.

Azzurri: The Italian international rugby team.

Baa-Baas: See **Barbarians**.

Backchat: Form of **dissent**.

Back row: The third row of the **scrum**. A collective term for the two **flankers** and **Number Eight**.

Back-three: Collective name for the two **wing three-quarters** and the **fullback**.

Backs: Division within the team whose prime role is to initiate attacking moves when in possession and to defend when opponents have the ball.

Ball boy: **Touchline** helper who collects balls that have been kicked out of play.

Ball-carrier: A player who has **possession** of the ball.

Barbarians: Famous Home Unions-based touring team with no home club or ground.

Barging: A **line-out** offence designed to unbalance a player who is about to jump for the ball.

Bench: The place outside the pitch where the **replacements** or **substitutes** wait before being called to take part in a match.

Binding: Name given to the way in which **forwards** grasp one another by wrapping their hands and arms around the body of a team-mate to stabilise a **scrum**, **ruck** or **maul**.

Bledisloe Cup: The trophy for which New Zealand and Australia compete.

Bleus (Les): The French international rugby team.

Blind side: The side of the field that is closer to the **touchline** at a set piece or a breakdown in play.

Blind-side flanker: The flanker who packs down on the **blind side** of a scrum.

Blitz defence: A method of defending that depends on players advancing quickly on their opponents, closing down space and inducing hurried play that leads to handling errors and a **turnover** of possession.

Blocking: A forward skill that prevents opposition **forwards** coming through at the **line-out**.

Blood bin: A place outside the pitch temporarily visited by a player for treatment for a blood injury.

Blood replacement: A player who comes off the **bench** and onto the pitch to temporarily replace a member of the playing XV who has a blood injury.

Blood reversal: A player who comes back onto the pitch after temporarily receiving treatment off it for a blood injury.

Blue: A player who has taken part in the annual Oxford–Cambridge University match.

Bomb: See **up-and-under**.

Bonus points: Points awarded in some tournament matches (e.g. the

Tri-Nations, the Heineken Cup) to teams that score four or more tries in a match and/or lose by seven or fewer points.

Boot money: Money paid to leading players – literally as a surreptitious wad of cash left in a boot or shoe – in the years before Rugby Union became a professional sport.

Boring in: A **scrum** offence perfected by **props** and difficult for referees to detect. The prop directs his shove inwards at an angle instead of square on to the opposition's **front row**.

Box: The blind-side area near touch behind a **set piece**, **ruck** or **maul**.

Box kick: A punt usually made by a **scrum half** from a **set piece**, **ruck** or **maul** that is hooked back to the **blind-side touchline** for a colleague to run on to.

Break (making a): Running with the ball and piercing the opposition's defence.

Breakaway: Australian term for a **flanker**.

Breakdown: A place where neither side makes progress – usually because of a **tackle** or because the ball goes loose – prior to a **ruck** or **maul** taking place.

Bridge: Name given to the body position adopted by a player who initiates a **ruck**. The player forming the bridge usually stands with legs apart over the ball and must have his shoulders higher than his waist when he makes contact with other players.

British and Irish Lions: See **Lions.**

Cabbage patch (Billy Williams'): Old nickname for Twickenham. Billy Williams was the RFU committee member who earmarked the site, which was originally a market garden and orchard, for development.

Calcutta Cup: The trophy for which England and Scotland compete. The cup, made from melted-down rupees, was presented on the dissolution of the Calcutta Club in India and has been played for annually since 1879. It is the oldest trophy in international rugby.

Call: A directional instruction given to the thrower at a **line-out**.

Can–Am: Name given to the annual match between Canada and the United States.

Canucks: Nickname for the Canadian national rugby side.

Cap: International match (or other representative level) appearance. So-called after the rugby custom of awarding a player who has appeared in such a match a velvet cap with tassel.

Captain: The player appointed to lead the team on the pitch.

Carry: A run made by a player while carrying the ball.

Catch and drive: A **line-out** move. Instead of feeding the ball to the backs, the catcher sets the ball for a **driving maul**. The **tactic** is usually used near the opposition's **goal line**.

Cavaliers: Unofficial New Zealand team who toured South Africa during the apartheid era (1986).

Celtic League: The leading annual competition for the Irish provinces and the Scottish and Welsh regions.

Centre: One of the two players in the middle of the four **three-quarters**.

Charge down (vb): To block, smother or deflect an opponent's kick without attempting to catch the ball.

Cherry Blossoms: The Japanese international rugby team.

Chip kick: Short **punt** aimed over a defender's head so that the kicker or one of his team-mates can run onto the ball and gather it before it strikes the ground.

Churchill Cup: Annual tournament featuring Canada, United States, England A and other invited national representative teams.

Cite: To name a player suspected of foul play.

Clearance: Any kick that relieves the pressure on the **defending team**.

Closing up: Illegal bunching by players in the **line-out**, closing the compulsory one-metre gap laid down in the laws as the required space between jumpers.

'Club': Nickname for Blackheath RFC, one of the original clubs in England.

Coach: Person who improves players' skills and advises on the team's tactics for a match.

Coarse Rugby: Informal version of rugby where players participate for social rather than competitive motives.

Collapsing: The illegal (and dangerous) act of deliberately disrupting **scrums**, **rucks** and **mauls**, for which the punishment is a penalty kick to the opposition.

Conversion: A **place kick** or **drop kick** at **goal** after a **try** has been scored.

Cook Cup: The trophy for which England and Australia compete.

Crash ball: A move where the ball-carrier tries to run through a would-be tackler like a battering ram, making no subtle attempt to beat his opponent.

Crash tackle: Driving **tackle** that stops a player with the ball in his tracks.

Crawshay's Welsh: Welsh invitation side run on similar lines to the **Barbarians**.

Crooked feed: Offence committed by a **scrum half** who does not feed the ball down the middle of the **tunnel** at a **scrum**.

Crossbar: The horizontal bar three metres above the ground between the vertical uprights of the **posts** and over which the ball has to be kicked in order for a goal to be scored.

Cross kick: Punt made by an attacking team from the **touchline** designed to be gathered in midfield by one of the kicking team's players.

Cross-field kick: Diagonal punt made by an attacking team designed to be gathered near the **touchline** by one of the kicking team's players.

Crossing: **Obstruction** in which a player runs directly in front of the path of a team-mate who is carrying the ball.

Crouch: First instruction in the sequence of four called by the **referee** when a **scrum** is awarded.

Crowning Years: Wales's unprecedented run of four **Triple Crown** successes from 1976 to 1979. Sometimes unkindly referred to (by non-Welsh followers of the game) as 'the crowing years'.

Currie Cup: Annual South African domestic tournament for the leading provincial sides.

Curtain-raiser: Southern hemisphere term for any event staged at a ground before the main rugby match of the day.

Cushion: A small lead.

Cut the line: Reduce the number of players (usually from seven to four) participating in a **line-out**.

Cut-out move: A move that involves a **cut-out pass**.

Cut-out pass: A **pass** from one player to another that misses out a player of the same side who is between them.

Dangerous play: An illegal act that puts an opponent in danger of serious injury.

Dead: State of the game when the ball is beyond the **field of play** or the referee has stopped play for an infringement.

Dead-ball line: Perimeter line running the width of the pitch.

Debenture scheme: Fundraising measure used to finance a building project such as a new rugby stadium. In return for his cash outlay, an investor buys the right to purchase tickets during a fixed term for matches at the stadium at the ruling price. The original outlay is returned to the investor at the end of the term, making it effectively an interest-free loan.

Decoy: A player whose position and actions indicate to opponents that he is about to play a part in an attack, when in fact the opposite is the case.

Decoy move: Any attacking move that involves a **decoy** player.

Defence: The team without the ball. Their job is to prevent the opposition breaking through.

Defending team: The team in whose half of the pitch play is taking place.

Deliberate knock-on: **Knock-on** that wilfully causes a breakdown in play. The punishment for this offence is a penalty kick to the non-offending team.

Detached player: One (usually a **forward**) who is not **binding** onto a **ruck**, **maul** or **scrum**.

Direct kicking to touch: Kicking that sends the ball into touch on the full – i.e. without bouncing in the **field of play** before crossing the **touchline**. Only permitted as a ground-gainer when the kick is taken by a defender who is inside his own **22-metre line**.

Disengaged player: A player who has detached his **binding** in a **scrum**, **ruck** or **maul**. This is not an **infringement** for as long as the player retreats behind the **hindmost** player.

Dissent: **Backchat** to the referee or any action that undermines an **official**'s decision.

Dive pass: Type of **pass** usually perfected by the **scrum half**. By launching himself into the air and towards the recipient, the passer hopes to impart greater speed to the ball.

Dribble: To move forward with the ball under the control of the feet.

Double movement: An illegal action – typically a second attempt to **ground the ball** over the opposition's **goal line** for a **try** – by a player who has been **tackled** short of the line.

Downtown (coll): Said of a **punt** that sends the ball a long distance straight down the middle of the field towards the opposition's **goal line**.

Drift defence: Method of defending that depends on players (usually the **midfield backs** or the **back row**) policing opponents so that the direction of attack drifts less threateningly towards a **touchline**.

Driving maul: A **maul** in which ground is made through a forward in possession driving forward while still bound to his team-mates.

Drop goal: **Goal** scored from a **drop kick**.

Drop kick: A **kick** made by dropping the ball from the hands and striking it at the moment it rebounds from the ground.

Drop-out: Method of restarting a game when an attacking player has sent the ball into the opponents' **in-goal area** where it is subsequently touched down by a defending player. The **drop kick** to restart is taken by the **defending team** from its **22-metre line**.

Dropping (the binding): **Dangerous play** by the **front row** at **scrums**. Typically a player will pull the hand(s) with which he is binding in a downward direction before releasing his binding altogether. The effect is to destabilise the **scrum** and send his opponent to the ground, causing a **collapse**.

Dummy: Feigned passing action designed to deceive an opponent in order to get past him.

Dummy runners: Players who run purposefully in order to deceive opponents into thinking that their path will define the line of an attack.

Eagles: Nickname for the United States national rugby side.

Early bath (take a) (coll): Leave the field early after being shown a **red card**.

Early tackle: An illegal **tackle** made on a player before he receives the ball.

Engage: Final instruction in the sequence of four called by the **referee** when a **scrum** is awarded.

Engagement: The sequence of four stages that **front rows** are instructed to observe before contact is made at the **scrum**.

European Challenge Cup: Competition for the second-tier of European clubs and provinces.

European Cup: See **Heineken Cup**.

Exiles: Name given to London club sides that cater for players whose allegiance is (usually) to a nation outside England – e.g. London Irish and London Welsh.

Extra time: Finite extension of playing time that is applied to tournament finals that finish as a draw after normal playing time. Typically the teams will play two additional periods of ten minutes each way in order to produce a winner. Not to be confused with **added time**.

Fair catch: Clean catch made inside the catcher's **22-metre line** from a kick by an opponent. The catcher has to shout '**Mark!**' when fielding the ball. The reward is a **free kick** to the catcher.

Feed: To insert the ball into the **scrum**.

Field goal: Southern hemisphere expression for a **drop goal**.

Field of play: Playing area contained within the **touchlines** and **goal lines**.

Fifteen: A rugby team.

Fifteen-man rugby: Entertaining form of the game in which all members of the team join together to play open, attacking rugby.

Fifteen-metres line: Broken line running the length of the pitch, fifteen metres from each **touchline**. The line defines the rear of a **line-out**.

First five-eighth: New Zealand term for the **outside half**.

First-phase possession: Ball won at a **set piece**.

Five-eighths: New Zealand term for the **outside half** and **inside centre**.

Five-metres line: Broken line running the length of the pitch, five metres from each **touchline**. The line defines the front of a **line-out**.

Five-metre scrum: See **Scrum-five.**

Five Nations: Name given to the annual **International Championship** involving the four **Home Unions** and France that took place between 1910 and 1999.

Flagposts: Markers placed along the **touchlines** to show the corners of the **dead-ball line** and **goal lines**. Flags are also positioned, about one metre back from the **touchline**, to show the positions of the **twenty-two**, **ten-metre** and **halfway lines**.

Flanker: One of the two **forwards** on the outside of the **second row** of the **scrum**.

Flat alignment: Formation in which a team's **midfield backs** and **wings** lie flat across the width of the pitch and close to the **advantage line**.

Flat-foot: To deceive an opponent by sleight of hand or a rapid change of direction, thereby causing him to pull up.

Fly half: See **outside half.**

Follow up (vb): To chase a kick made by a player of one's own side.

Foot race: A race for a **loose ball** – usually lying in the **in-goal** areas – that involves a defender and an opponent.

Foot rush: Open play in which the ball is **dribbled** forward.

Foot-up: **Scrum** offence when the **hooker** strikes for the ball before it has been fed into the **tunnel**.

Forward pass: Minor **infringement** where a player propels or throws the ball in the direction of his opponent's **goal line**.

Forwards: Division within the team whose prime role is to win the ball at **set pieces** or retain possession when the game breaks down.

Foul play: Any action by a player that is contrary to the spirit of the game. Examples include **dangerous play**, misconduct, **unfair play**, unsporting behaviour, **retaliation** and **repeated infringement**.

Free kick: An award against a team for certain **infringements** or a reward made to a team making a **mark.**

From the side: Illegal direction of entry to a **ruck** or **maul**.

Front-five: The five tight **forwards** comprising the **front row** and two **locks** in the scrum.

Front row: The three **forwards** who form the first row of the scrum. **scrum**.

Fullback: Position of the last line of **defence**.

Full house: Name given to a scorer's accumulation of **points** if it comprises all four **scoring actions: try, conversion, penalty goal** and **dropped goal**.

Gain line: Another term for the **advantage line**.

Gallaher Cup: The trophy for which France and New Zealand compete. Named after Dave Gallaher, captain of the original All Blacks of 1905–6, who were the first team ever to play France in a rugby international.

Game plan: See **tactics**.

Gang-tackle: Legal simultaneous **tackles** on a ball-carrier made by two or more players.

Garryowen: Alternative name for an **up-and-under**. Named after the Irish rugby club that first used the move as a **tactic**.

Get out of jail (coll): Said of a player or team that recovers from a mistake or from a difficult position.

Goal [1]: H-shaped structure in the middle of the **goal lines** at each end of the **pitch**.

Goal [2]: Name given to scoring actions that involve kicking the ball by either a **drop kick** or **place kick** over the **crossbar** and between the **posts**.

Goal [3]: A converted **try**.

Goal lines: The lines through the goalposts running the width of the pitch.

Going to ground: Action of a tackled player who has been unable to **offload** the ball.

Golden era: Any extended period in the history of the game during which a team – particularly an international side – dominates its regular opponents.

Golden Oldies: Name given to past players who, after the age of 35, continue to compete in special rugby tournaments that are arranged by age group.

Go North: Direction taken by Rugby Union players transferring to Rugby League . . . the north refers to the North of England, Rugby League's traditional stronghold.

Grand Slam: Bridge term used since 1957 by the rugby press to describe the team that wins every match in the **International Championship**.

Ground the ball: Touch the ball down in the **in–goal** area.

Grubber kick: Short **punt** aimed deliberately downwards so that it skims the ground but bounces unpredictably into the path of the kicker or one of his team–mates.

Guest side: A team specially invited to take part in a rugby tournament.

Haka: Cultural dance and war cry laid down as a challenge by New Zealand rugby teams prior to their matches.

Half: Period of play that usually lasts 35 or, at senior level, 40 minutes.

Halfback: Player or players occupying a position between the **forwards** and **three-quarters**.

Half-time: Break or pause in the middle of a game before teams change ends for the **second half**.

Halfway line: The line running the width of the pitch equidistant from the two **goal lines**.

Halves [1]: The two **halfbacks**.

Halves [2]: The two periods over which a match takes place.

Handling in the ruck: Illegal act by a player in the ruck.

Hand-off: Legal use of the hand made by a player while carrying the ball to fend off an opponent.

Hands out: Call made by referees to discourage players from **handling in the ruck**.

Harpastum: Ancient Greek/Roman ball game thought to be the forerunner of rugby.

Heavy traffic (coll): Expression used to describe a concentration of players around a ball-carrier.

Heel: **Hooker's** method for winning the ball in **scrums**.

Heineken Cup: Leading tournament for European clubs and provinces. Rugby's European Cup.

Held up: Said of the situation when a player in **possession** crosses the **goal line** but is unable, through the efforts of the opposition, to **ground the ball** over the line for a **try**.

High tackle: An illegal **tackle** that is aimed above an opponent's shoulder.

Hindmost foot: The back foot or feet of the player in a **scrum**, **ruck** or **maul** that is nearest to his team's **goal line**.

Hit (coll): A **tackle**.

Holding on: Not releasing the ball in the **tackle** (see **not releasing**).

Home Unions: The collective name for the national sides and Unions of England, Scotland, Ireland and Wales.

Hooker: Middle **forward** in the **front row** of the **scrum**.

Hooter: See **siren**.

HQ: Informal name for Twickenham – the headquarters of the **RFU**.

Impact player: A substitute who is capable of changing the course of a match.

Infringement: Any action that contravenes the **laws** of the game.

In-goal: Area behind the **goal lines** where **touchdowns** are made.

Injury time: See **added time**.

Inside centre: The **centre** who positions himself so that he is always nearest to his **outside half**.

Inside half: See **scrum half**.

Inside pass: Pass made by a player back in the direction from which he has run.

Intentional knock-on: See **deliberate knock-on**.

Interception: A **turnover** of **possession** made by a player catching a pass made between opponents.

International [1]: Top level at which matches are staged.

International [2]: A player who has played at **international** level.

International Championship: Annual tournament dating from 1883 in which each of the four **Home Unions**, with later France (from 1910) and more recently Italy (from 2000), plays each other.

International Rugby Board (IRB): Body that runs and promotes Rugby Union worldwide.

Interval: The **half-time** break.

Invincibles: Name given to the 1924–25 All Blacks who won all 32 matches of their tour to Britain, Ireland, France and Canada.

IRB: See **International Rugby Board**.

Kick [1]: To propel the ball with any part of the lower leg from knee to toe but excluding the heel.

Kick [2]: To strike an opponent (usually illegally) with any part of the lower leg.

Kickoff [1] (n): The start (or restart after a score or half-time) of a match.

Kickoff [2] (n): Appointed time for the start of a match.

Kick off [3] (vb): To **drop-kick** the ball from the middle of the **half-way line** to start or restart a match.

Knock-on: A minor **infringement** where a player fails to control the ball with his hand or arm and knocks it to the ground in the direction of his opponent's **goal line**. A **scrum** follows with the non-offending side rewarded with the feed.

Lansdowne Cup: The trophy for which Ireland and Australia compete.

Last quarter: The final twenty minutes of a match.

Late charge: An illegal charge made on a player who has just kicked the ball.

Late tackle: An illegal **tackle** made on a player who has just kicked or passed the ball.

Lateral running: The tendency of an attacking move to drift sideways towards the touchline instead of forwards and over the **gain line**.

Laws: The rules of the game.

Lay the ball back: The action of a tackled player who immediately makes the ball available to his supporting team-mates.

Lazy running: Deliberate attempt to disrupt the flow of the game made by players apparently retreating from offside positions.

Leaning: A **line-out** offence.

Left wing: The **wing** who positions himself so that he is always nearest to his left **touchline**.

Lifter: The **forward** – usually a **prop** – whose role is to lift a jumper in the **line-out**.

Lifting: Support given to jumpers at the **line-out**. The help is legitimate provided the support is above the waist and takes place after the ball has left the thrower's hands.

Line break: A **break** that takes a team beyond the **advantage line**.

Line-kicking: **Kicking** aimed to gain ground by finding touch.

Line of touch: Imaginary line running the width of the pitch and through the middle of the **line-out**.

Line-out: **A set piece** for restarting the game after the ball has gone into **touch**.

Line through a mark: A line through a given point and running parallel to the **touchlines**.

Lions: Name given to the team of players that represents the four **Home Unions** on tours to South Africa, New Zealand or Australia.

Lock: One of the two **forwards** in the centre of the **second row** of the **scrum**.

Loitering: Deliberate delay to return onside by a player in an **offside** position.

Long throw: Legal **line-out throw-in** that travels above the heads of the forwards and beyond the **fifteen-metres line**.

Loose ball: The ball's state when neither side is in **possession**.

Loose forward: A **flanker** or **Number Eight**.

Loose-head: The **prop** who plays on the left side of the **front row**.

Loose play: **Phases** of the game that fall between the **set piece** and **open play**.

Lying on the ball: An offence that prevents clear passage of the ball at a **tackle**.

Manager: The head **coach**; the person responsible for all aspects of a team's preparation.

Maori: Aboriginal New Zealand rugby player.

Marching orders (coll): Instruction given to a player who is **sent off**.

Mark: A claim made for a **free kick** by a defender who catches the ball cleanly behind his own **22-metre line** after it has been kicked by an opponent.

Maul: The form that a breakdown in play takes when one or more players from each team (who must be on their feet) are in physical contact with a player carrying the ball.

Middlesex Sevens: Annual **sevens** festival staged at Twickenham for club and **guest** sides.

Midfield backs: Collective name for the influential trio comprising the **outside half**, the **inside centre** and the **outside centre**.

Mini-rugby: Non–contact variation of rugby for young beginners. Emphasis is on running and handling with the aim of scoring **tries.**

Mitts: Fingerless gloves worn by some **backs**.

Narrow side: The **blind side**.

Near side: The **blind side**.

Nelson Mandela Plate: The trophy for which South Africa and Australia compete.

New cap: A player who makes his first appearance for his province or country.

Nobody home (coll): A defence that is caught out of position.

No-side: The final whistle indicating the end of a match.

Not releasing: The illegal delay in releasing the ball after a **tackle**.

Not straight: Said of a **crooked feed** into the **scrum**.

No. 10: Shirt number worn by the **outside half** and hallowed in Wales, the nation noted for producing outstanding players in the position.

NPC championship: New Zealand's principal domestic senior rugby tournament.

Number Eight: The rearmost **forward** in the **scrum**.

Numbers (coll): Commentator's call when a team in possession has a potential **overlap**.

Oaks: Nickname for the Romanian national rugby side.

Obstruction: The illegal interference with an opponent who is playing within the spirit of the game.

Offensive defence: Any form of defence that relies on the old maxim: 'attack is the best form of defence'.

Official: Collective name for the **referee**, **touch judge** or **TMO**.

Offload: A **pass** made by a player who is being tackled.

Offside: Offence whereby a player strays beyond an imaginary line defined by the rearmost feet of his own forwards at a **scrum**, **ruck** or **maul** – or ten metres from the **line of touch** at a **line-out**. In general play, players are offside unless they remain behind the ball when it has been played by a team-mate.

Offside line: An imaginary line defined by the rearmost feet of a player's forwards at a **scrum**, **ruck** or **maul** – or ten metres from the **line of touch** at a **line-out.**

Old Bill: Nickname given to the **Webb Ellis Trophy** by Australia's **Rugby World Cup** winning team in 1991.

Old fart (coll): Derogatory term for an **alickadoo**.

One-cap wonder (coll): Player who made only one appearance for his country.

On-the-line: The convention in rugby football is that, if a ball lands on a **touchline** or is touched down on a goal line, it is regarded as being behind that line for law interpretations.

On your feet: Warning call made by referee to players, particularly at the **tackle**.

Open: Term used to describe Rugby Union's release (in 1995) from its strictly amateur code.

Open play: **Phases** of the game in which running and passing are to the fore.

Open side: The wider part of the pitch available at a set piece or a breakdown in play.

Open-side flanker: The flanker who packs down on the **open side** of a scrum.

Original offence: An **infringement** from which an **advantage** to the non-offending team might accrue. If the advantage is not immediate, the referee will return to the original offence to restart the game.

Originals: Name given to the first New Zealand side that toured Britain, Ireland, France and North America in 1905–6.

Outside centre: The **centre** who positions himself so that he is always between the **inside centre** and the **open-side wing**.

Outside half: One of the two **halfback** positions in a team. Also known as the out-half (in Ireland), stand-off half or fly half.

Out-half: Expression commonly used in Ireland for the **outside half.**

Overcooked (coll): Description of a kick that travels too far – directly into touch from outside the kicker's **twenty-two** or over the opponent's **dead-ball line** – effectively gaining no ground at all.

Overhead pass: Type of **inside pass** in which the ball is thrown from above the passer's head.

Overlap: Situation in **open play** when an **attacking team** outnumbers the defence.

Overstep: To fall **offside** by stepping over the **offside line** (with one foot or both) at a **set piece**, **ruck** or **maul**.

Pacific Islanders: Collective name given to the international rugby teams of Fiji, Samoa and Tonga.

Pack: Collective name for the **forwards**.

Pack leader: The player appointed to lead the **forwards**.

Pass (vb): To propel the ball from one player to another by hand.

Pass (n): Movement of the ball by hand from one player to another (usually of the same side).

Pause: Third instruction in the sequence of four called by the **referee** when a **scrum** is awarded.

Peel off: Move involving the front-row and second-row forwards running back after a **throw-in** to support a catcher who initiates an attack from the tail of a **line-out**.

Penalty goal: **Goal** scored from a **penalty kick**.

Penalty kick: Penalty against a team for certain types of **infringement**.

Penalty try: **Try** awarded when the **referee** believes one would have been scored but for an infringement by the **defending team**.

Phase: A passage of play.

Piano-players (coll): The **backs** – players who fall under the spotlight in the running and handling game that typifies **open play**.

Piano-shifters (coll): The **forwards** – players who beaver away in the **set pieces**, **rucks** and **mauls** performing their arts away from the spotlight.

Pick-and-go (or *pick-and-drive):* Move launched (usually by the **Number Eight**) by picking up the ball as it emerges from a **scrum** or **ruck**.

Pile-up: Ineffective **ruck** that finishes in a mass of bodies smothering the ball.

Pill (coll): The ball.

Place kick: A kick at **goal** taken after the ball has been placed (and remains stationary) on the ground.

Placer: Non-kicker who steadies the ball (in windy conditions, for instance) in preparation for a team-mate to take a **place kick**.

Play to the whistle: Instruction given to all players: never anticipate the referee's decisions.

Ploy: Move launched by **forwards peeling** from a **line-out**.

Pocket (in the): Position occupied by a **receiver** who stands deep behind a **set piece**, **ruck** or **maul,** usually to give himself time and space to make a clearing kick or drop for goal.

Points: Means by which a team increases its score.

Possession (in): Said of the team that has control of the ball.

Posts: The upright parts, just over five and a half metres apart, of the **goal**.

Pot: Expression for a **drop kick** at goal.

Powergen Cup: Tournament featuring the Anglo–Welsh professional clubs and regions.

PRA: The Professional Rugby Players' Association. The professional body that protects players' interests in England.

Premier Rugby: Umbrella organisation that represents the twelve clubs in the English **Premiership**.

Premiership: The top division for the twelve leading English club sides.

Professional game: Originally a term to describe **Rugby League**, where payment for playing the game was permitted. Now used to describe the parts of the Union game that embraced professionalism when the **IRB** declared it open in 1995.

Prop: A player either side of the **hooker** who provides support in the **front row** of the **scrum**.

Pulling down: A dangerous and illegal action that causes a **scrum**, **ruck** or **maul** to collapse.

Pumas: Nickname for the Argentinean national rugby side.

Punt: A type of kick in which the ball is dropped from a player's hands and struck by the foot before it touches the ground.

Pushing: An offence that interferes with an opponent jumping for the ball at a **line-out**.

Pushover try: A **try** that results from a drive at a **scrum, ruck** or **maul** that takes a player in control of the ball over the opposition's **goal line**.

Put-in: **Scrum** feed.

Quick ball: **Possession** that is transferred at speed from the forwards to the backs.

Quick hands: Accurate **passing** that results in the swift transfer of the ball in **open play**.

Quick throw-in: **Throw-in** taken before teams take up their usual line-out positions.

Quintuple Tie: Unique result to the **International Championship** of 1973 when each of the **Five Nations** won two home games but lost their two away games.

Rake (n): Southern hemisphere term for a **hooker**.

Raker: A long, low kick that is usually aimed towards the **touchline**.

Ranfurly Shield: Challenge competition involving the senior New Zealand provincial sides.

Receiver: The player – usually the **outside half** – who is the first to receive a **pass** from the **set piece, ruck** or **maul**.

Red card: Card shown by a referee when a player is to be permanently sent from the field for misconduct.

Red zone: The period when a match has entered **added time**.

Referee: The official who controls the play on the rugby pitch.

Repeated infringement: Constant and usually deliberate contravention of the same law. The ultimate sanction for this offence is a sending off.

Replacement: A player who comes off the **bench** and on to the pitch to replace an injured member of the playing XV.

Restart: The **kickoff** after a score or at the start of the second half.

Retaliation: Illegal reprisal taken by a player who has been infringed against – usually before the referee has had the chance to act on the original **infringement**.

Retention (of the ball): Keeping **possession**.

Reverse pass: To propel the ball behind one's back to reverse the direction of an attack.

RFU: See **Rugby Football Union**.

Ride (vb): To escape a **tackle** or manage to **offload** the ball while being tackled.

Right wing: The **wing** who positions himself so that he is always nearest to his right **touchline**.

Rolling maul: A **maul** in which ground is made through a forward in possession rolling off the back of a **maul** and driving forward while still bound to his team-mates.

Round-the-corner: Place-kicking style in which the kicker takes a curved run-up before striking the ball with his instep.

Route one (coll): Short straight run into an opponent taken by a player (usually a **front-five forward**) carrying the ball.

Ruck: The form a breakdown in play takes when one or more players from each team (who must be on their feet) are in physical contact closing around the ball when it is on the ground.

Rugby Football Union (RFU): The organisation that administers and promotes the game in England.

Rugby League: Thirteen-a-side version of rugby, set up in the 1890s as a professional breakaway from the then strictly amateur Union game.

Rugby World Cup: A four-yearly tournament played by the senior international teams of the member Unions of the **International**

Rugby Board.

Rush defence: See **blitz defence.**

Russell Cargill Trophy: The trophy awarded to the winners of the **Middlesex Sevens**.

Saxons: Name given to the England A team, the sub-international side.

Scissors: A move that involves the ball-carrier and a colleague running at a sharp angle across each other's path. If the ball-carrier passes to his colleague, the direction of the attack is considerably altered. The move can also involve a **dummy** – tricking the opposition into believing that the ball-carrier's colleague will receive a pass when in fact the carrier retains the ball.

Scoring action: Collective name for the actions that yield **points** – **try, conversion, penalty goal** or **dropped goal**.

Screw kick: See **torpedo kick.**

Scrum: **Set piece** for restarting the game after certain infringements.

Scrum cap: Protective headgear – usually worn by **forwards**.

Scrum-five: A **scrum** that takes place five metres from the **goal line** with the **feed** awarded to the **attacking side**.

Scrum half: **Halfback** who provides the link between the **pack** and the **backs**. Also known as the inside half.

Season: Period of the year during which Rugby Union is played. In Britain, Ireland and Europe this currently runs from September to May. In the southern hemisphere the season runs from February to October.

Second five-eighth: New Zealand term for the **inside centre**.

Second half: Second and final period of a rugby match.

Second-phase possession: Ball won at a **ruck** or **maul**.

Second row: The four **forwards** who form the middle rank in the **scrum**.

Sent off: The end of a match for a player who has been shown a **red card**.

Series: Sequence of **international** matches (usually two or three in number) between the same two nations.

Service: General description of the passing link between a **scrum half** and **outside half**.

Set piece: Collective name for **scrums** and **line-outs**.

Sevens: Shortened version of Rugby Union played on a full-size pitch but between teams of seven on each side.

131

Shamateurism (coll): Term used to describe the culture of illicit payments made to players in the amateur era before Rugby Union officially became a professional sport in September 1995.

Shepherding: American football–style of blocking (to protect a ball-carrier). The action is an **obstruction**.

Shin pad: Protective item of kit used by **props** and **hookers** to protect their shins in **scrums.**

Shoeing (coll): Illegally trampling over the body or legs of a player who is lying near the ball or in a **ruck**.

Short side: The **blind side**.

Sideline: See **touchline**.

Sidestep: Rapid change of direction of a runner in order to get past an opponent.

Sin bin: The place outside the **field of play** where a player who has received a **yellow card** sits out his temporary exclusion from the game.

Siren: Hooter that marks the end of playing time in each **half** of a match.

Six Nations: The name given to the annual **International Championship** involving the four **Home Unions**, France and Italy that has taken place since 2000.

Skipper: See **captain**.

Slow ball: Possession that is delivered very slowly from the **forwards** to the **backs**.

Spear tackle: Dangerous and illegal **tackle** in which the tackled player is turned and thrown headfirst towards the ground.

Spin pass: Type of **pass** usually perfected by the **scrum half**. By rolling his wrists quickly over the ball as it leaves his hands he usually achieves greater length on his pass.

Springboks: Nickname for the South African national rugby side.

Stamping: Dangerous and illegal use of the boot on a player who is lying on the ground.

Standing deep: Formation in which a team's **midfield backs** and **wings** lie diagonally across the width of the pitch and deep behind the **advantage line**.

Stand-off half: See **outside half**.

Static maul: A **maul** that makes no ground and results in the side in possession **turning over** the ball for the opposition to feed the ensuing **scrum**.

Stay on your feet: Golden rule for players in or about to join **rucks** and **mauls** – advice often given by **referees** during the course of a match.

Steal: An unexpected **turnover** in **possession**.

Stoppage: Any pause in play.

Straighten the line: Correcting **lateral running** in attack by directing it forwards and over the **gain line**.

Straight out: Description of a touch kick taken from beyond a player's 22-metre line and which crosses the **touchline** before bouncing, resulting in a **throw-in** back where the kick was made.

Strike: The hooker's action when he tries to win the ball for his side at a scrum.

Studs: Sprigs on the soles of players' boots that provide grip.

Sub-international: First level of match importance after **international** level.

Substitute: A player who comes off the **bench** for tactical reasons to replace a member of the playing fifteen.

Success rate: Percentage of successes out of attempts at **goal** made by a team's **place-kicker**.

Super: Prefix referring to the leading sub-international tournament played annually by the top provincial sides in the **Tri-Nations**. In 2007 the tournament became the Super 14, having been known as the Super 12 for a decade or so before that. The number refers to the number of teams taking part.

Super Saturday (coll): A match day that features three (or more) big matches in succession, especially on the final round of a televised tournament such as the **Six Nations**.

Sweatband: Bandage worn around the forehead by **forwards**.

Swerve: Arcing run used by a player to outflank an opponent.

'Swing Low, Sweet Chariot': Anthem of England's rugby supporters. First heard at Twickenham when England beat Ireland in 1988, their coloured wing Chris Oti scoring three tries.

Tackle (n/vb): To stop a player with the ball, usually by wrapping arms around the player's legs and bringing him to the ground.

Tackler: Player who makes a **tackle**.

Tactics: Plans conceived by a team or a player that decide how a side or individual will play the game.

Tail: The back of a **line-out**.

Take (n): A clean catch made by a player in the **line-out**.

Take an early bath (coll): Go off permanently to serve a **red-card** punishment.

Tap-and-go: A quick **free kick** or **penalty** in which a player taps the ball forward and picks it up himself.

Tee: A device used to steady the ball when players prepare for a **place kick**.

Ten-man rugby: Dull **tactics** adopted by a team that relies exclusively on its eight **forwards** and two **halfbacks** to make use of **possession**. The remaining five **backs** are only called on for defensive duties.

Ten-metre line: Broken lines running the width of the pitch ten metres either side of the **halfway line.**

Ten-metre law [1]: Minimum distance at which players not participating in the **line-out** must stand from the set piece.

Ten-metre law [2]: **Law** that permits referees to penalise players or teams who backchat or deliberately delay play when a **penalty** or **free kick** has been awarded. The non-offending team will take the kick ten metres closer to the offending side's **goal line**.

Teros: Nickname for the Uruguayan national rugby side.

Territory: Statistical measure of a team's domination. It measures the percentage of a match that a team has spent in its opponent's half.

Test: International match – especially one of a **series** of games between the same two nations.

Three-quarter line: Collective description for the **three-quarters**.

Three-quarters: The four players occupying positions between the **halfbacks** and **fullback**.

Through-the-gate: The approach route players must take when joining the **ruck** or **maul**. The imaginary gate is the position of the back foot of a team-mate who is already bound on. Anyone joining must bind on from a position behind that critical foot and from a direction parallel to the **touchline**.

Throw-forward (n): A **forward pass**.

Throw-in: Action taken when play restarts with a **line-out**. The ball must travel at least five metres and along a path perpendicular to the **touchline**.

Tight game: **Phases** of play in which **set pieces, rucks** and **mauls** are to the fore.

Tight-head: The **prop** who plays on the right side of the **front row**.

Time on: Call made by the referee to restart the clock after a **stoppage**.

Time-out: Call made by the referee when he wants the clock stopped while he speaks to the players or while an injured player receives attention (not to be confused with the time-out in some sports, e.g. American football, that can be called by the team coach).

Tipping: An illegal and dangerous act deliberately disrupting **line-out** jumpers for which the punishment is a penalty kick to the opposition side.

TMO: The television match official. Expert called on to adjudicate **try** decisions when the **referee** is uncertain.

Toe kick: Place-kicking style in which the kicker takes a straight run-up before striking the ball with his toe.

Torpedo kick: A type of **punt** that sends the ball spiralling towards the **touchline**.

Toss: Spin of the coin that takes place between the rival captains before a match takes place. The winner decides which team takes the kickoff or which end of the ground it will defend for the first **half**.

Touch (n): The area outside the **field of play** bounded by the **touchlines**.

Touch (vb): Second instruction in the sequence of four called by the **referee** when a **scrum** is awarded.

Touchdown: Act of touching the ball down behind the **goal line**. A player who does this behind an opponent's line scores a **try**.

Touch-in-goal: The extensions of the **touchlines** beyond the **field of play** from **goal line** to **dead-ball line**.

Touch judge: Official responsible for signalling when the ball has crossed the **touchline** or passed over the **crossbar** at a place kick at goal, and who assists the referee in cases of foul play.

Touchline: Perimeter line running the length of the pitch.

Tour: Any visit undertaken by a rugby team for the purpose of playing a sequence of matches away from its home.

Tourist: Player chosen to take part in a rugby **tour**.

Tramlines: The two broken lines near **touch** – the **five-metres** and **fifteen-metres lines** – that run the length of the pitch. The area between the tramlines is occupied by forwards participating in **line-outs**.

Trampling: Illegally treading on the body or legs of a player who is lying on the ground.

Tricolores: Nickname for the French national rugby side. See also **Bleus**.

Tri-Nations: Collective name for the national sides and Unions of New Zealand, South Africa and Australia.

Triple Crown: Trophy awarded to the **Home Union** that wins all three of its matches against the other Home Unions.

Truck-and-trailer (coll): When sides make progress at the **maul**, the player in possession must be bound to colleagues beside him or, in the case of a **driving** or **rolling maul** to those in front of him. If the players in front become unattached from the ball-carrier, there is an obstruction – the truck is said to have become detached from the trailer.

Try: Scoring action worth five **points**.

Tunnel: The imaginary middle line of the **scrum** directly beneath the shoulders of the **front rows**.

Turned (of a tackled player): When a player is **tackled** he will usually try to place the ball so that it is between his body and his own **goal line**. This makes the ball readily available for his team-mates and usually ensures possession from the ensuing **ruck** or **maul**. The opposition, however, will try to turn the tackled player so that the ball lies between him and their own goal line, making **turnover possession** more likely.

Turned through ninety degrees: Description of a **scrum** that has rotated through a right angle before the ball emerges. The **referee** will blow his whistle and reset the **scrum** for another **feed**.

Turnover: Win possession from the opposing side.

Twenty-two, or 22-metre line: The lines running the width of the pitch twenty-two metres from each **goal line**.

Two-on-one: **Overlap** situation in which a ball-carrier with a colleague free outside him is faced by only one defender.

Two-tackler system: Method of defence in which two defenders are detailed to **tackle** an attacking player simultaneously.

Uncontested: Said of a **scrum** where one of the sides is unable to field a fit **front row**. The **forwards** are not allowed to push and the side feeding the **scrum** is the only one that is allowed to **strike** for it.

Under the cosh (coll): Description of a **defending team** that is under sustained pressure.

Unfair play: An illegal act where a player deliberately contravenes the spirit of the game or wilfully infringes the laws.

Union: National body responsible for the organisation of the game within a nation.

Up-and-under: A kick where the ball is sent very high into the air.

Upright [1]: The vertical part of a goalpost.

Upright [2]: Ineffective **scrum** position where a **front row** is unable to pack low.

Upstairs (going) (coll): Said of a referee's decision to consult the **TMO**.

Use it or lose it: Maxim governing **mauls**. The team in possession must use the ball – either by maintaining forward momentum or recycling it. If the maul becomes static and the ball does not emerge, a scrum put-in will be awarded to the side not in possession.

Varsity match: Annual Twickenham match between Oxford and Cambridge Universities.

Viet Gwent: Nickname of the much-vaunted Pontypool and Wales **front row** of the 1970s.

Wallabies: Nickname for the Australian national rugby side.

Webb Ellis Trophy: The prize awarded to the nation that wins men's senior Rugby World Cup.

Wheeling: Rotating a **scrum** before the ball emerges. See **turned through ninety degrees**.

Whistle: **Referee**'s action to halt a match.

White-line fever (coll): Selfishness shown near the opposition's **goal line** by an attacking player who tries in vain to score himself when he has team-mates available in scoring positions.

Wide game: A **tactic** that aims to spread the ball quickly to the team's **wing three-quarters** and stretch the opposition's defence.

Wing: One of the two players on the outside of the **three-quarter line**.

Wing forward: See **flanker**.

Working over (coll): Using the feet to clear bodies or the ball in a **ruck**.

Wrap-around: A move that involves players overlapping behind the backs of the ball-carrier.

XV: A **fifteen**.

Yellow card: Card shown by a referee when a player is to be temporarily sent from the field for misconduct.